fi...
with
meditation

Naomi Ozaniec

flash.

For UK order enquiries: please contact Bookpoint Ltd, 130 Milton Park, Abingdon, Oxon OX14 4SB. *Telephone*: +44 (0) 1235 827720. *Fax*: +44 (0) 1235 400454. Lines are open 09.00–17.00, Monday to Saturday, with a 24-hour message answering service. Details about our titles and how to order are available at www.hoddereducation.com

British Library Cataloguing in Publication Data: a catalogue record for this title is available from the British Library.

First published in UK 2011 by Hodder Education, part of Hachette UK, 338 Euston Road, London, NW1 3BH.

Typeset by MPS Limited, a Macmillan Company.

Printed in Great Britain for Hodder Education, an Hachette UK Company, 338 Euston Road, London NW1 3BH, by CPI Cox & Wyman, Reading, Berkshire RG1 8EX.

The publisher has used its best endeavours to ensure that the URLs for external websites referred to in this book are correct and active at the time of going to press. However, the publisher and the author have no responsibility for the websites and can make no guarantee that a site will remain live or that the content will remain relevant, decent or appropriate.

Hachette Livre UK's policy is to use papers that are natural, renewable and recyclable products and made from wood grown in sustainable forests. The logging and manufacturing processes are expected to conform to the environmental regulations of the country of origin.

Impression number   10 9 8 7 6 5 4 3 2 1

Year   2015 2014 2013 2012 2011

Contents

Preface

The Western meditation in which you are invited to share is a unique pot-pourri. Purists might indeed frown upon its eclectic nature, absence of lengthy training and informal organization, but this is indeed a new movement, it is Aquarian in every way. Organic and self-defining, it has none of the rigid structure of a defined and stratified hierarchy. What it lacks in age it compensates for in inventiveness, creativity and discovery. It is the genuine and spontaneous response to the deepest call of our times for personal meaning. This homegrown movement has produced its own gurus, John Gray, Caroline Myss, Jean Houston and Deepak Chopra, among many others, who teach not in the temple but through the workshop and best-selling books, cassettes and videos.

The wisdom that is being voiced is directly related to daily life, not temple life, and to the everyday issues of health, happiness, relationships and all that is encompassed by the world at large. The outstanding figures in the new generation of Western teachers bring gifts from the traditions in which they served as apprentices. Such teachers have distilled and redefined traditional practices for a new generation living out in the world bearing all the pressures of careers, relationships and family life. John Gray, author of the best selling Venus and Mars series, is in many ways typical of the new Western guru. As a celibate Hindu monk for nine years he spent more than ten hours in daily meditation. Now this unlikely candidate has poured a new wisdom into the tired institution of marriage and has revitalized our understanding of what a loving relationship can be. His clarity, truthfulness and insight has healed thousands of relationships and enabled everyday folk to find meaning in life. He is typical of the new style of teacher. He is totally grounded in spiritual practice and offers you a personal wisdom so that your life might benefit. You do not need to join anything, give up anything other than limiting beliefs, take up any religious practice or adopt a particular lifestyle. What he brings is the revitalizing power of the new idea. So potent is the power of an idea whose time has come that, when he spoke on Oprah Winfrey's show, 30 million people tuned in to hear him. His message through the medium of mass communication provides a perfectly framed Aquarian moment: global communication enables a new idea to be disseminated freely to the massed mind. Western teachers appear in unexpected places and guises. Oprah herself has become a true inspiration for so many, women especially. She is a powerful model of personal transformation. Speaking in the language of today she draws upon a wellspring of timeless spiritual wisdom and embodies the possibilities of a transformed life. With some notable exceptions, women have been denied a voice within the oldest traditions. Now, perhaps for the first time, women have become spiritual teachers and will bring a powerful understanding to the newly emerging wisdom stream. It was John Lennon who gave us the phrase 'Power to the People'. How right he was. This has become the time for personal and collective empowerment. The process is ongoing and self-seeding. This is indeed the dawning of the Age of Aquarius whose characteristics are communication, technology, revolutionary ideas and the emergence of the family of humanity. This is the full nature of the revolution in hand.

The religious traditions of the world have each become rich repositories of human possibilities. The infinite variety of prayer and praise, song and sound, icon and architecture is a bountiful harvest. The mindset of separation, however, is ultimately divisive and sets one path against another in righteous fervour. The mindset of unification brings diverse paths together with respect and in recognition of each other. Separation is now giving way to unity as boundaries dissolve through the medium of communication and exchange. The book, the video and the Internet have opened a doorway into the great religions of past and present. The temple walls have become transparent. The outside world may peer in and the inside world may see outwards. In this new time renouncing the world is no longer essential in order to find the spiritual life. The path to the spiritual life is on your doorstep.

Spiritual intelligence

The heart of the spiritually intelligent self is, ultimately, the quantum vacuum, the ground of being itself. It is a still and changing ground, and the heart knows it is the still and changing heart.

Danah Zohar and Ian Marshall, *Spiritual Intelligence*

In the vortex of the current revolution, normally unrelated areas are finding a common cause at the cutting edge: physics and mysticism, creativity and technology, neurophysiology and psychology and religion and science are all finding unexpected concord. As we move towards a more holistic framework, the hard and fast boundaries that we historically took upon ourselves now appear to be imprisoning rather than useful. New models are free to emerge when the straightjacket of dogmatic thinking and ideological conformity is loosened.

The new concept of spiritual intelligence (SQ) has emerged from the holistic marriage of a grounding in the humanities combined with the scientific measure of up-to-date brain research. The result is a new perspective on who we are. The authors, Danah Zohar and Ian Marshall define SQ as 'the soul's intelligence, it is the intelligence with which we heal ourselves and with which we make ourselves whole'. This new concept is radical. The word 'spiritual' is sometimes conveniently diminished to describe those whimsical attitudes and irrational choices that lead to opting out rather than opting in. But SQ gives us the concept of a practical and internalized working guidance, which is indispensable to our real needs. So how can SQ help us in daily life? When do we draw upon it? According to the authors, 'SQ is our compass "at the edge", life's most challenging existential problems exist outside the expected familiar, outside the given rules, beyond past experience, beyond what we know how to handle... It is the place where we can be at our most creative. SQ, our deep, intuitive sense of meaning and value, is our guide at the edge. We use SQ to reach forward towards the developed persons that we have the potential to be. SQ helps us to outgrow our immediate ego selves and to reach beyond to those deeper layers of potentiality that lie hidden within us.' A person high in SQ is described by the authors as 'a servant leader', a wonderfully paradoxical term that perfectly describes the transformed self. If SQ is defined as 'our ultimate intelligence' do you already have it? Do you want it? How can you develop it? What are you willing to give up in order find your own SQ? It is perhaps salutary to reflect on the notion that the ways and means to develop SQ have always been available under many different guises. Historically, seeking the unconventional, the hidden and the esoteric in times and places geared to but one convention and mode of thought might mean persecution, even death. Today, at last, the ways and means of developing SQ are free to all.

To gauge your existing SQ, ask yourself the following questions:

Do you have:
* The capacity to be actively flexible and spontaneously adaptive?
* A high degree of self-awareness?
* A capacity to face and use suffering?
* A capacity to transcend pain?
* The quality of being inspired by vision and values?
* A reluctance to cause harm?
* A tendency to see the connections between diverse things?
* A marked tendency to ask 'why' or 'what if' questions?
* A faculty for working against convention?

Meditation brings the capacity to be actively flexible and spontaneously adaptive. It creates a high degree of self-awareness. Meditative practice never shies away from the real issues of human suffering but provides ways and means through its lonely labyrinth. Meditation awakens us to the possibility of being inspired by vision and values. It presupposes a reluctance to cause harm and takes us on a journey to a deeper and unified reality where the connections between diverse things become apparent.

Introduction

The gift of learning to meditate is the greatest gift you can give yourself in this life.

Sogyal Rinpoche, *Meditation*

There can be no doubt that interest in meditation continues to grow as ordinary people struggle to make sense of increasingly complex and hectic lives. It is clearer than ever that personal meaning will never be found in the technological accoutrements of contemporary life, no matter how exciting such tools appear to be. Technological mastery is no provider of well-being or peace of mind. Material goods offer a seductive and short-lived satisfaction to those who gain them and serve as a bitter disappointment to those who seek them without success. Technology and materialism are here to stay; these are the driving forces of contemporary society. We cannot change our own history, but we can find a greater vision where these twin powers have a place, but do not rule. When every waking moment has become consumed by consumerism, when the still voice of the heart has been drowned out by imagined glitz and glamour, we have paid too high a price for comfort, ease and security. When the sense of being trapped by the treadmill becomes overwhelming, we know we have failed to strike a healthy balance in our lives. When the relentless passing of time seems to diminish, rather than expand our opportunities for enrichment, who will not cry out 'There must be more to life than this!'

In the West, meditation has proved popular as an antidote to our stressful lives. But meditation practice is not simply a remedy for overwork and the ailments of contemporary life. This use is merely an offshoot from a much sturdier tree. Meditation is not relaxation, though it is often confused with it. Meditation is not therapy, though it has therapeutic applications. Meditation is not an excuse for introspection, but a process of expansion. Meditation is a means of complete personal transformation. Such phrases convey little initially, rather as a description of a foreign and rarely-visited land might entice but not really inform the novice traveller. Let the idea become an invitation to initiate your own transformation. Travel yourself and discover the meaning behind the words.

There can be no doubt that meditation originated and flowered in cultures and societies very different from our own. We have little in common with the mountains of Tibet or the monsoon of India. We are worlds apart from the rice fields of Asia and the landscape of Japan. Yet we share a common imperative as human beings, namely to know ourselves. The East has a long and constant meditative tradition. The West has found meditation sporadically. Currently the West is looking to the East as a source of inspiration, while at the same time attempting to develop methods and approaches that suit the circumstances of our lives. We are hoping to draw fresh water from a deep well of ancient wisdom.

Yet we need to remember the very great differences between these two cultures. In the East, where generations of monks have walked and taught, spiritual needs are recognized as legitimate human expressions. The spiritual life is simply integrated into the fabric of life through long established temples, shrines, ashrams and monasteries. There is a sense of balance between the spiritual and the material, the earthly and the eternal. In India, it is acceptable for a man to devote the first half of life to the duties of family in the capacity as householder, but to renounce these same duties and become the spiritual seeker in the second half of life. This acknowledges both the material and spiritual dimensions of life. Moving from the mundane to the spiritual recognizes the healthy mid-life transition. When this is not recognized, it so often afflicts the soul and becomes a mid-life crisis. When mainstream culture sees spiritual commitments as being both normal and real, attending to such needs becomes unremarkable.

In the West, we still nurture a certain suspicion that a sense of spiritual commitment is somehow beyond the norm and not fully real. In the East, the spiritual is honoured by mothers and fathers, grandparents and children. It is part of perfectly normal life. Spiritual expression is simply integral to life. In the West, 'the spiritual' is still treated as something 'other'. Our schismatic mindset is ever operative. Pioneering thinkers, spiritual therapists, travellers, the bold and the insatiably curious have brought meditation to us only by going beyond Western confines, both physical and cultural. Such rich food has been seized upon by the spiritually disenfranchised, the disappointed and the eternally hopeful. Integration is still to come. There can be no doubt that East and West represent two quite different realities by every possible definition. It would not be unfair to note that the East has developed a spiritual life at the expense of the material life, while the West has developed a material life at the expense of the spiritual. Perhaps both East and West have something to give the other.

Who can fail to recognize the spiritual vacuum in our midst? Orthodox religion is fast losing its hold. The whirlpool of change is drawing upon the old and the new, the ancient and the modern, the radical and the traditional. We sense a profound and sometimes frantic attempt to establish a new footing in a rapidly changing world. Activity and massive interest may mask our uncertainty; experimentation has become our hallmark, while the East looks on unruffled.

Meditation beckons us like nourishment to a starving man. It has stood the test of time. We sense our predicament. We recognize the imbalance at the heart of our shared lives. We know that we have served mammon only too well. It is time to redress the balance. It is time to look within. We in the West have lived in the outside world for long enough. Though we may look to the East, it is to ourselves that we must ultimately look. No amount of borrowing or interpretation of ancient texts compensates for a society long divided between the spiritual and the material. Visits by Buddhist Lamas, Zen Roshis and Yogic Gurus serve to remind us of the gaping hole in the fabric of Western culture. As we look towards meditation we come to examine the very values, principles and beliefs that have sustained Western civilization for so long.

Meditation is not a secular activity; we cannot escape this basic fact. Meditation has developed within the broader context of the great spiritual traditions of the world. This does not mean that we should equate meditation with any particular religious belief. We need to make a distinction between the exoteric and the esoteric face of any organized religion. The exoteric body transmits those specialized teachings, codes of behaviour, relevant laws, practices and observances that uphold a particular social, cultural and religious identity. This is the religion of the masses where there is a place for everyone. Within the exoteric religious body there exists an esoteric heart. This is the place of spiritual experience, not social gathering. It is the active path of personal transformation, not the place for handed-down dogma. It is the path for the few. The Sufi Way preserves the inner tradition within Islam. *Kabbalah* provides the inner path within Judaism. Christianity has its mystical side too. The many paths of Yoga represent yet another esoteric tradition. Within Buddhism the esoteric and exoteric have not become separate identities but remain intertwined.

While we find great divergence of belief and intent between the religions of the world, we find a remarkable unity throughout the esoteric traditions. We find ourselves standing at the outer door in the hands of our parents. We arrive at the inner door by our own efforts because we have deep and burning questions. We stand with many questions and much confusion. We hold a vague sense of the spiritual. We feel unsatisfied with the answers we have been given throughout life. As we pause at this threshold we may either return or proceed. If we proceed we will find that both responsibility and commitment are placed firmly in our own hands. Self-knowledge and self-awareness lie ahead. Our questions will have a place but the answers will come not from the intellectual and rational mind but from the expanded consciousness, insight and the seeds of wisdom, which are the hallmarks of the meditative mind.

beginning – the first step

1

Regular meditation will bring you beneficial change, in mind, body and spirit. As a gentle chain reaction is set in motion, beneficial change will spread into the many areas of your life: your inner resources will unfold, your sense of connection with everyday life will deepen, your openness to others will flower, your intuition will strengthen, your mind will become clearer, your aspirations and goals will change, your self-confidence will grow and you can move away from a damaging past and recast the future. These psychological and spiritual qualities form the foundation for personal well-being, health and happiness. Even though meditation is not therapy, its effects are often therapeutic and the medical profession has already come to see its many benefits. You will be able to see the results for yourself. Give yourself the gift of meditation and take your life in a new direction.

Getting ready

It is wisely said that the journey of a thousand miles begins with a single step, so let us begin. Your journey towards meditation will take shape as you find yourself this very day. This path will be built within your life as you find it now. The practice of meditation will arise from your own needs, aspirations and intentions. The life that is yours today is like a seedbed in which you have chosen to plant the possibility of meditation. Your behaviour, attitudes, values and commitment will determine whether this seed dies or flourishes. People come to meditation for many differing reasons. It can begin out of curiosity or as a dimly felt need. It can commence as a purely intellectual interest or an antidote to stress. It is sometimes triggered by a crisis. More often it is the end result of a long process of discontent and dissatisfaction with the goals offered by society. It is possible to be successful, financially independent, surrounded by the trappings of family and career and yet still feel empty. Some people just have an instinctive feeling that there is more to life than just a succession of experiences.

From the outset it should be understood that meditation touches the whole life and the whole person. Therefore the first step towards meditation consists of taking stock of the person we are today, of the life we have today and of the whole situation in which we find ourselves. This is no idle suggestion but a serious request and an opportunity to build your future meditation practice on a firm foundation. Please, take some time for personal reflection. What factors have led you towards meditation? What hopes and expectations do you have? Do you feel ready to plant the seed of meditation in your life? Are you willing to be changed through meditation? What characteristics would you consider to be important as a foundation for a spiritually based life? Let there be no mistake – the practice of meditation is derived from the monastery and the ashram. It may have travelled into the outside world with good effect, but it remains the spiritual discipline par excellence. We should not make the mistake of attempting to separate the practice of meditation from the life in which it is lived.

We should not forget that meditation has always been part of a wider spiritual life. Meditation is an integral aspect of all Buddhist and Yogic practice. Taking the practice out of its wider context is not without difficulties. By contrast, meditation remains undeveloped in theory and practice within mainstream Western spirituality. Despite the fact that we find relatively few deep cultural hooks to which we may attach practice, we seek meditation with sincere heart and genuine need. We may profitably look to the older, long established traditions of the East, while at the same time bearing our own cultural and spiritual circumstances in mind. This particular period offers great opportunities. Meditation is not static, but dynamic. The West has its own needs, and recognizing and meeting our needs may legitimately give rise to new forms of ancient principles. Meditation can take many forms, as history shows. Through time, practice has evolved as enlightened teachers have arisen and nourished the tradition that nourished them. There can be no doubt that meditation is a living stream. The West may drink deeply here too.

At this point we may profitably look at the principles that sustain Buddhist and Yogic practice. Both the Noble Eightfold Path of Buddhism and the Eight Limbs of Yoga provide a context in which meditation can take root. If we do not set meditation within the context of a whole life, we make the fundamental mistake of believing that we can simply add practice to daily life without truly making the space to incorporate and integrate its effects. There are some noteworthy similarities between the Noble Eightfold Path and the Eight Limbs. In each case a moral framework precedes meditation practice. Both traditions establish clear moral ground rules that cover behaviour in all forms – social, moral and ethical. Buddhism sets out the Five Precepts, which expressly forbid killing, stealing, sexual misconduct, lying and taking intoxicants. Yoga commences with the Five Yamas, which are non-violence or non-injury, truthfulness, not stealing, chastity and non-acquisitiveness. Both traditions build the practice of meditation upon a period of moral and ethical preparation. A period of preparation has value that should not be overlooked. In our present culture of moral relativism, we are ready to ignore the idea of a preliminary moral training. Yet this always precedes Eastern practice. As a result Westerners are ill prepared for the psychological changes that rightly take place during the period of preparation. Meditation, which is the development of consciousness and the discovery of a deep one-pointed state of mind, can only truly arise from the moral life.

The spiritual path

If you wish to know the road up the mountain, you must ask the man who goes back and forth in it.

Japanese proverb

It is common to speak of the spiritual life as a path. This metaphor has value as it gives us the idea of a journey with a beginning and a destination. It is also comforting to realize that we are not alone and that others have trod this same path before us. The idea of the path is established most strongly in the East, where monastic communities have a long history. In such specialized environments a shared language evolved naturally. Generation after generation ensured continuity through lives of study, practice and discussion. The path is a natural consequence of long lived continuity. Buddhism offers the Lam Rim, which is the graduated path to enlightenment. Hinduism recognizes diversity in unity and it offers several avenues: the *Karma Marga* is the Path of Action; the *Bhakti Marga* is the devotional path; the *Jhana Marga* is the Path of Knowledge; and the *Virakti Marga* is the Path of Renunciation. These various avenues recognize that individuals bring different temperaments to the spiritual life.

We can begin to unravel the complexities of meditation by drawing upon the familiar image of a target. In other words, thoughts will be aimed at a particular target. We find this notion in the Judaic tradition through the classical Rabbinical term for mental concentration, *kavvanah*, which is intentionality. The word is derived from *kaven* meaning 'to aim'.

Focused awareness: the path of concentration

Although at first our concentration may be very brief, if we persevere in the practice it will progressively lengthen.

Geshe Rabten, *Treasury of Dharma*

Using the idea of a target in the mind, it is easy to see that our intention is to strike as near to the bull's eye as often as possible. This is, of course, much easier said than done, as anyone who has tried will know. Nevertheless, we should not be disheartened by early failure. The difficulty of this apparently simple task has been recognized by the sages and spiritual teachers of all times. In the *Bhagavad Gita*, Arjuna says, 'The mind is so relentless, inconsistent. The mind is stubborn, strong and wilful, as difficult to harness as the wind.' It does not take long to discover the truth of this statement. Soon enough, we come face to face with our own mental clutter, our boredom, our resistance and our inability to concentrate. As we set out on the journey towards meditative practice, it may be that we are considering the qualities of mind for the first time. There is much to discover and much to learn. Geshe Rabten describes meditation as 'a means of controlling, taming and eventually transforming the mind'. This ambitious goal begins in the simplest way; we begin to develop a more focused awareness. This includes a level of sustained concentration and additionally contains an element of self-observation. Using the mind in this way is quite different from everyday awareness, which makes no attempt constantly to review itself. A simple exercise will introduce you to the idea of one part of the mind watching another. Watch the stream of your own consciousness by observing your own thoughts.

The first attempts to focus our awareness often prove to be disheartening. Unwanted thoughts arise as if from nowhere. Developing this skill as a sustained and reliable ability will take time and effort. It will not happen in a week, it will not happen without frustration. It will not happen without personal commitment. The advice from the experienced is universally gentle and comforting: don't give up, just carry on. Don't get involved in your thoughts, just let them pass. Return the mind to the subject of the meditation, the target. Allow other thoughts to flow through. Stay focused. Stay aware.

Focused awareness clearly demands a development in concentration. Unfortunately this particular quality still smacks of the classroom and enforced learning, which is not helpful. Too often we associate concentration with mental strain, intense effort and difficulty. Concentration is not an end in itself but the necessary precondition that excludes distractions and diversions. Without concentration, no subject for meditation can be held in the mind. Geshe Rabten sets out six similes of concentration, which enable us to extend the concept of meditative concentration to include qualities of calmness, constancy, dynamism, clarity and lightness.

Subjects for meditation

Everything can be used as an invitation to meditation.

Sogyal Rinpoche, *Meditation*

We do not need to look to the arcane and the distant but to the ordinary and the present for meditation subjects. Meditation is considered to be a means of uncovering the true nature of the human being. Practice therefore often commences with ordinary human activities such as breathing and moving. Awareness is focused on these mundane activities. Daily activities serve as the target for the opening of the meditative mind. The breath is followed universally as a subject for meditation. It is, after all, an obvious and simple choice. Focused awareness becomes mindful as we take in more and more everyday activities. We begin to live mindfully instead of mindlessly as we attempt to notice what we are doing as it happens. So much of daily life is automatic and neglected. Meditation brings awareness into ordinary life.

In complete contrast to the detached observation of natural processes, meditative practice may also focus on created visualized images. Meditation can take place on a single symbol or a constellation of symbolic images. The symbolic offers a rich vein for meditative and contemplative thought. Symbols serve to expand consciousness and develop the qualities of insight and intuition. Symbols can be presented for meditation through innumerable forms. Sometimes a physical representation is used, at other times the image is just created with one part of the mind while it is simultaneously contemplated. Symbolic paintings, constructions, stories, statues, sacred objects, treasured icons and even imagined realities all serve to transform the mind.

Particular symbolic traditions have evolved, as certain forms have become regularly employed. The **mandala** is a circular symbolic representation of both universal and personal forces. It is employed in a particular way for meditation. The traditional Tibetan mandala is drawn according to a symbolic schema and approached through a long established convention.

The **yantra** is another visual representation but it uses geometric shapes to represent cosmic and personal connections. The *Shri Yantra* is composed of nine interpenetrating triangles, which symbolize male and female energies. It represents the whole of creation.

The Judaic mystical tradition is unique in representing a complex philosophy entirely in symbolic form. This is a most remarkable interplay between philosophy and symbol. The single embracing image, **Otz Chiim** or the Tree of Life, contains a host of interconnected symbols. Here is a lifetime's study and meditation.

Subjects for meditation are varied and endless, traditional and emergent, widely different yet unified in purpose.

Although certain subjects have become traditional through extended use, we should not feel confined by the past or intimidated by the learned. Sogyal Rinpoche takes meditation right into the heart of daily life. He reminds us to be inventive, resourceful and joyful as we take the openness of the meditative mind into the everyday world: 'A smile, a face in the subway, the sight of a small flower growing in the crack of a cement pavement, a fall of rich cloth in a shop window, the way the sun lights up flower pots on a window sill. Offer up every joy, be awake at all moments.' Subjects for meditation are everywhere.

2

opening –
the inner
frontiers

The Cycle of Meditation

The Cycle of Meditation enables us to view meditation as a continuous and dynamic process. Meditation is a process, not an isolated event.

Preparation: posture

Sit, then as if you were a mountain with all the unshakeable, steadfast majesty of a mountain.

Sogyal Rinpoche, *Meditation*

Meditation begins with sitting. It is common to think that meditation begins with relaxation. But it is important not to confuse the two states. Entering relaxation serves more as a demarcation between the outer busy world and the inner state that we are seeking. Although it is not uncommon to formally relax as preparation for meditation, this stage should eventually be dispensed with so that meditation can be entered directly.

There is no doubt that the full lotus position is still favoured by the classical meditative traditions. In this position the foot of the right leg is placed over the left thigh and the foot of the left leg is placed over the right thigh. However, this is a difficult position for most people. Less strenuous variations are possible, but these also require a level of suppleness which may well prove too difficult. In the half-lotus position, one foot lies on the opposite thigh while the other foot rests under the opposite thigh. In the quarter-lotus position, while one foot lies under the opposite thigh, the remaining foot lies under the opposite leg. All these crossed-leg postures present difficulties for many Westerners; we are just not used to sitting in this way. It is of course possible to work towards these positions if you choose, but daily work on the muscles of the thighs and legs, ankle joints and feet is required. If these classical positions are beyond you, take heart that other much easier positions are also suitable. In the traditional Japanese kneeling posture, a cushion relieves pressure on the heels. This kneeling position can also be used on a low bench with padded seat.

As meditation becomes integrated into your life, you will find that it becomes natural to move into the meditative mind wherever you are and sitting becomes a matter of choice.

Application: the subject of the meditation

If we do not control the mind, we will achieve nothing.

Geshe Rabten, *Treasury of Dharma*

After the stage of preparation is complete, the subject of the meditation is brought to mind. This is our target. Whether the subject is our own breath, a symbol, a phrase or an idea, our intention is to return to it over and over again. Although the mind will still wander, the target serves to keep us focused. The process of learning to stay on target requires patience and perseverance. It fosters the development of mental awareness and leads to mental self-control.

Realization: the fruit of the meditation

Many have come to realization simply by listening to the tinkling of a bell or some other sound.

Roshi Philip Kapleau, *The Three Pillars of Zen*

Every meditation is like a seed planted in the mind. In time it will bring forth its own fruit. Nothing particular may be apparent on the surface after each meditation but something imperceptible has taken place. The fruit of the meditation is the gain, the realization, the distilled nectar. It is the essence of our inner work and the culmination of our efforts. It may take many forms. There may be a changed conscious understanding or a realization about your own life in general. The culminating realization may come as a dream, in a moment of sudden insight or through a symbol revealed to the inner eye. It may come as a thought or as a non-thought, as a feeling or as a knowing. Be open to all possibilities in yourself. Be aware and you will see the fruit of the meditation ripening. You may even catch it as it falls.

Transformation: the effect of the process

The faculty of continual transformation ... is a profound expression of the dynamic character of the mind.

Lama Govinda, *Creative Meditation*

This aspect of the process is less easy to identify on a day-to-day basis. We tend not to see ourselves changing; others may see it first. Personal change can sometimes be dramatic but it is most often gradual and organic. This is the most reliable and best way. All too often people come to meditation with unfounded expectations. They hope for the dramatic, the bizarre and the extraordinary. This will not happen. 'The real miracle', as Sogyal Rinpoche points out, 'is more ordinary and much more useful. It is a subtle transformation and this transformation happens not only in your mind and your emotions but also actually in your body.' Meditation works at a very deep and potent level. It is working even when we do not see anything happening. Once the process has commenced it is self-sustaining. It works much like the body's own natural processes. Body cells are renewed constantly, yet we see no change. The body is transformed continuously by day and by night. Meditation enables us to experience a total transformation gently and quietly from within the depths of being. So if you take up meditation with a good heart and sincere intent, expect to be changed.

Meditation: the way of change

It is not easy for us to change. But it is possible and it is our glory as human beings.

M. Scott-Peck, *The Different Drum*

Change follows regular meditation as surely as night follows day. So do not be surprised when change begins to happen for you. It is impossible to look ahead and see how meditation will work for you. It works at so many levels simultaneously. Meditation brings physical, emotional and intellectual changes, which can culminate in a deep and lasting change that might well be termed a spiritual awakening.

The degree to which you will be changed by meditation depends on many factors, including your own need for change. Only you can decide what you need from practice and how much time you will give to it. At the outset, be prepared to be changed as you journey.

Meditation and physiology

Meditation is commonly promoted as an antidote to stress. Nowadays this idea is accepted and acceptable but this was not always the case – this notion was once quite radical. It was during the 1970s that scientific method was first applied to meditation. Research discovered that meditation produced observable physical changes in a number of parameters. It was observed that meditation effected a lowered metabolic rate, which uses less oxygen and produces less carbon dioxide. The lactate concentration of the blood was noted to be decreased during meditation. This was a significant finding as blood lactate level is related to anxiety and tension. Another significant discovery was the noted correlation between meditation practice and specific brainwave patterns. There were some spectacular encounters with yogis and experienced meditators, which showed that consciousness outstripped our ability to measure it. The book *The Relaxation Response,* published by Herbert Benson in 1975, highlighted the therapeutic benefits of the deeply relaxed state. This discovery spawned new approaches in mental and physical treatment programmes. Relaxation began to be used to good effect with patients suffering from high blood pressure and stress-related disorders. Research continued into the 1980s and, in 1984, the US National Institute of Health released a consensus report that recommended meditation along with salt and dietary restrictions above prescription drugs as the first treatment for mild hypertension. Researchers found that meditation decreased the body's response to norepinephrine, a hormone indicated in cardiovascular stress. Relaxation has been found to help conditions of angina and arrythmia and to assist in the lowering of blood cholesterol levels. There is still much to learn about the body/mind.

Meditation and spirituality

Meditation works directly with consciousness. In doing this, we are inevitably taken into the fundamental area of human existence. We work directly with the mind from within. We step into the alchemical furnace of becoming. We come to work with ourselves in depth and finally we come fully to realize ourselves. This sharpens the spiritual quest, which is not undertaken as some vague existential adventure, but under a directive to know ultimate nature. On the journey into the nature of being human, much will transpire.

The meditation journal

Newcomers to meditation are most likely to work alone. It is very easy to feel isolated and uncertain. In the Western tradition, it is common for students to keep a personal meditation diary. Perhaps this stems in part from the historical precedent found in the Judaic tradition where the practice of diary keeping has long been advised. Rabbi Joseph Karo, a sixteenth-century mystic, kept a diary for more than 30 years. His contemporary Rabbi Chaim Vital kept a detailed dream diary. The Midrash relates that the patriarch Jacob kept a log of significant events, including the dreams of his son Joseph. This is a helpful practice, most especially to newcomers.

Begin your journal with all the things that you hope meditation might help you find. This initial list will help to establish your starting point. In the future you can look back to see how far your experience measured up to your expectations. You may also discover that your expectations themselves changed through your experience. In any event, your first thoughts about meditation are of personal value, so record them. Journal keeping encourages self-discipline and strengthens personal commitment. However, the journal is not the place for lengthy introspection, but for brief and succinct reports, which attempt to distil every practice to its essence. Get into the habit of writing your notes immediately after the session while the ideas are fresh in your mind.

3

establishing – the integrated life

Historically there has been a deep divide between the spiritual and the secular life, but at this time of spiritual renaissance there is a great desire to take the gifts of the spiritual life into a secular setting; meditation is the bridge between these two worlds. This is a time of great change and meditation has its part to play in the newly emerging global paradigm. The regular practice of meditation gradually brings mind, body and spirit together in harmony. Conscious awareness brings purpose and peace to daily life, personal relationships and life choices, mindfulness is the antidote to robotic thinking and, like an anchor, it integrates everything we do. The shared task of our times is the need for integration between the spiritual and the secular, separation belongs to the past. Today the spiritual life can be created in the exchanges and interactions of daily life mindfully lived.

I cannot say it strongly enough: to integrate meditation in action is the whole ground and point and purpose of meditation.

Sogyal Rinpoche, *Meditation*

The divide between what is perceived to be spiritual and what is perceived to be material is deeply rooted in Western culture. This stilted theology has run its course. It has taken a heavy toll in the oppression of the human spirit. The notion of separation has become so culturally ingrained as to be invisible, but we feel its effects. We sense the sterility of a life cut off from nature, we feel a sense of intangible loss and we simply realize that something is out of balance in our lives as individuals and in the wider group. Eastern philosophies have never lost a sense of holism. The flesh and the spirit, the world and the divine, manifestation and the Absolute have never become estranged any more than two sides of the same coin. If we keep the mundane and the holy apart, we are merely perpetuating an idea that has served its time. The new frontiers of physics show us more clearly than ever that the manifestation of life is baffling, mysterious and amazing. Matter holds many secrets. We are now searching for holism with all the appetite of a starving person seeking food. There is currently an instinctive desire to reunite body and spirit, heart and mind, the mundane and the supramundane. We are now looking for the very bridges, whether symbolic, psychic or practical, which were severed in the attempt to isolate the spiritual from life itself. Meditation constitutes such a bridge. It resolves the polarities that appear to be separate and reconciles the paradoxes that life presents. We are immersed in the paradoxical, the great and the small, the incomparably vast and the impossibly tiny, natural beauty, human cruelty, human courage, natural disaster, the timeless and the passing of time, human birth, human death and all that passes in between.

All meditative systems promote self-awareness and detached observation as a means of watching our inbuilt preconceptions and value judgements. Zen simply asks us to see the 'isness' of things, in other words to see things as they are without the added gloss of our own projected imaginings. This seems absurdly simple. The contemporary teacher Osho gives simple advice:

You look at a flower – you simply look. Don't say 'beautiful',
'ugly'. Don't say anything. Don't bring in words, don't verbalize.
Simply look. In the beginning it will be difficult but start with
things with which you are not too involved – look at things
which are neutral – a rock, a flower, a tree, the sun rising, a bird
in flight, a cloud moving in the sky. Start from neutral things
and only then move towards emotionally loaded situations.

Denial, deception and delusion

If I ignore it, maybe the problem will go away.

Everyday thought

Denial, deception and delusion are everyday realities to the
therapist. This is the baggage that we accrue as we travel through life.
The longer we carry these three inner demons, the heavier our burden
becomes and ridding ourselves of them becomes increasingly difficult.
Therapy is a common route. The therapist acts in the capacity of a
detached witness by holding up a mirror to our behaviour. Meditation
is a less common route. Through meditation we can learn to function
in the capacity of a detached observer and hold up a mirror to our own
behaviour. In doing this we take an important step towards weaving
spiritual values and the ordinary life into one seamless garment.

Without some degree of conscious awareness we remain
prisoners of early conditioning and upbringing. We carry behaviours
and ingrained responses into later life like invisible millstones. In the
interchange of close relationships, we approach every encounter
with an array of complex predispositions and long-standing ways
of behaving. These personal patterns are the hardest to identify
as they have become invisibly embedded within us. Yet like ruts
in a riverbed our long established expectations determine
reactions and responses. We experience the moments of everyday
life through the lens of our own construction. If we have low
self-esteem, we may feel constantly criticized, and if we are deeply
fearful, we cannot trust. If we are lacking in confidence, we may
compensate by exuding an air of bravado. Self-justification, passing
responsibility and blaming others all permit us to use denial in

our own defence. We can deny the big faults and the small faults, we can deny cause and effect, we can deny responsibilities and involvement. The awakened meditative mind, however, permits no such denials, for in the clear light of day self cannot hide from self. Denial will thrive wherever the status quo carries weight. We avoid seeing things as they are and warp the turn of events to maintain the illusion that favours our perspective. We scapegoat others to safeguard ourselves. Though we recognize the truth at some deep hidden level, the truth may be too hurtful to acknowledge openly. Difficult relationships breed self-deception as blame is thrown back and forth. We hide from the truth to protect an image we hold of ourselves. Delusion, denial and deception are the common currency of everyday life and relationships. When we are ready to admit the light of awareness, we are ready to find ourselves.

Meditation enables us to develop a watching consciousness; it enables us to give birth to the watcher within. Buddhism names six root delusions and 20 secondary delusions. Looking at these takes us straight back to ourselves, for there is no other place to be.

The six root delusions

1 Attachment: our attachment to objects exaggerates and distorts. Things seem desirable and we will spend much effort and energy in order to own or gain the object of our desires. This mental factor is difficult to eliminate.

2 Anger: anger destroys peace of mind and is harmful to the body. However, it is easier to subdue as we cannot fail to be aware of it in our lives.

3 Pride: through pride we exaggerate our own status. We want to feel special and important in some way. We believe we are superior to others. Prideful people find it very difficult to seek help from anyone. Pride is a great obstacle to the development of the mind as it brings an attitude of mental closure.

4 Ignorance: this is considered to be the root of all delusions. It is likened to the root of a poisonous tree that produces only rotten fruit. Ignorance can only be overcome through personal effort and conscious work.

5 Negative doubt: this refers to aspects of the negative results of doubting the validity of Buddhist teaching. It is likened to someone who sets out with the intention of building a machine but soon doubts its value and ceases to work on the project rather than complete the task.

6 Mistaken views: this refers to the way in which the philosophical views we take direct behaviour and action. Mistaken views result in extreme or harmful acts, such as mortification of the body.

The root delusions named by Buddhism are the nitty-gritty of the world in which we live and move and have our being. The first four of these root delusions are the common human experiences. Who has not experienced one if not all of them at one time or another? Who has not encountered spite, jealousy and avarice? Who has not felt lack of confidence or been inattentive? The 20 secondary delusions present a long list of human frailties well known to us all. They are belligerence, vengefulness, concealment, spite, jealousy, avarice, pretence, dissimulation, self-satisfaction, cruelty, shamelessness, lack of regard for others, mental dullness, excitement, lack of confidence, laziness, unconscientiousness, forgetfulness, inattentiveness and distraction. The central questions are simple. Do we wish to continue to experience pretence, self-satisfaction and forgetfulness in ourselves? Do we wish to change aspects of ourselves? Are we willing to experience change? Are we open to the possibility of change? Do we have the commitment to implement change? These are the central questions of the integrated life, which is the ordinary life lived through the light of self-awareness.

Mindful living

Mindfulness is the miracle by which we master and restore ourselves.

Thich Nhat Hanh, *The Miracle of Mindfulness*

'Mindless vandalism' is a phrase that we all recognize and understand. It means to act without thinking, to destroy for no reason, to function unconsciously. The phrase 'mindless living' may not be the stock-in-trade of the press but we can apply it all the same. What is mindless living and how can we avoid it?

Buddhism sets great store on the development of mindfulness. It is the complete opposite of mindless living. It offers specific practices. Mindfulness covers several areas: mindfulness of breathing, mindfulness of the body, mindfulness of mental content, and states of both mind and feelings. Don't let these lengthy titles mislead. These practices are neither obscure nor esoteric; they apply perfectly to the situations of everyday life. The Vietnamese monk and writer Thich Nhat Hanh understands the needs of ordinary life. He knows the pressures of everyday life:

> *One must prepare projects, consult with the neighbours, try to resolve a million difficulties; there is hard work to do. You might well ask: how then are we to practise mindfulness. My answer is keep your attention focused on the work, be alert and ready to handle ably and intelligently any situation which may arise – this is mindfulness.*

Here is the union of practice and ordinary life. Here is the integrated life in the making.

Mindfulness of breath is central to mindfulness in life, just as the breath is central to life itself. The breath can be employed in many ways. Become aware of your breath and make it your friend. Try lying down flat without a pillow, place one hand on your stomach and one hand on your upper chest. Breathe deeply and slowly until you are aware of the relationship between stomach, lungs and diaphragm. Next you can measure the length of your own breath by counting in your mind. You can then extend the length of the inhalation or exhalation. All these simple exercises develop your concentration and awareness.

The same principle of paying close attention is also applied to other aspects of daily life. When developing mindfulness of feeling, we watch our reactions and responses to external stimulus on a moment-to-moment basis. Accordingly, we note how things make us feel, whether pleasant, unpleasant or indifferent. When developing mindfulness of bodily posture, we pay close attention to our own movement on a moment-to-moment basis.

The phrase 'Know Thyself' takes on a new meaning in the light of mindfulness practice. How mindful are you? How mindfully do you live?

Daily awareness

The objective is to be in awareness, you must simply be aware of what you do when you are doing it, not afterwards.

Shaykh Fadhalla Heari, *The Sufi Way to Self Unfoldment*

Meditation begins in a small way as a practice of perhaps five to ten minutes. Eventually it merges with every aspect of daily life so that you develop a daily awareness of everything in your life.

Practice becomes life and life becomes practice. Awareness can be thought of as whatever you notice on a moment-to-moment basis. Living without awareness is to sleepwalk through your daily routine, but living in awareness is to be awake in life. Direct awareness is simply seeing things as they are. This is quite different from drawing upon book learning, acquired knowledge, possible theories, plausible explanations or any other intellectual constructions. Direct awareness is just about looking and seeing without embellishment. 'While sitting, I make almost no use of my intellect', writes Thich Nhat Hanh. It seems very curious that we have to practise continuously in order to develop what should be most natural to us, that is, perceiving the world about us.

Paying attention means just seeing things as they are without embellishment or overlay. This breaks down our categorizing habits. Each object is merely itself. Moreover, giving attention to the unfolding moments of daily life serves as a brake on our wilder passions, flights of fancy and rash decisions that arise in the heat of the moment and then deflate like burst balloons in the cold light of day. Paying attention to the moment frees us from both the past and the future. How much time is wasted daily as we relive past encounters and anticipate future outcomes? Live in the moment with awareness. Set about establishing the integrated life for yourself.

4

deepening –
the way of the
heart

The sensitivities of the heart, compassion and loving kindness are innate human qualities which can easily become swamped and forgotten in the busy world. However, in recent decades there has been a return to a gentler and holistic spirituality, and the many movements for spiritual regeneration now place personal and shared value on the way of the heart once more. Meditation takes place through the conscious intent of the mind but at the same time the sensitivities of the heart are opened; compassion and kindness naturally blossom as mind, body and spirit awaken. The humanizing qualities of the awakened heart have value not just for the individual but for society at large, since it is the heart which acknowledges the universal equality of each person. The present spiritual renaissance is taking practical meditation into fundamental organizations: education, health, and business, where awareness of others is seen to bring a communal benefit.

The more the heart is an avid void, the more abundantly light will shine into it.

Thich Nhat Hanh, *The Sun My Heart*

The knowing heart

Who do you care for? Who do you love? Who loves you? You know the answer to these questions with a certainty that needs nothing more. The heart knows, it is as simple as that. It is not surprising that many cultures have identified the seat of the soul with the heart. In these times we seem to have lost contact with the knowing of the heart and the seat of the soul. We are mystified by the mystical and shy at talk of the soul. Instead, we value the cold rationalization of the intellect. We fear the knowing of the heart. It defies logic. The spiritual traditions of the world have each kept the flame of the heart alive in their own way. Even when the practice falls short of the ideal, the ideal remains. Christianity is perceived as an outflowing of love to the world. Buddhism is based on the generation of compassion. The heart takes us beyond the confines of the self towards a universal realization of connectivity. It takes us beyond rationality, which knows nothing of love.

Opening the heart

The opening of the heart is rarely accompanied without personal suffering and pain. The rose with its thorns universally symbolizes the trials and pains of love, both personal and mystical.

The Sanskrit word for compassion is *karuna*, which is derived from the root *kr*, which implies action. Indeed, how can true compassion exist without the impulsion to act? Service might be thought of as compassion in action, though this might be thought rather old fashioned in today's fast moving world. If the concept of service appears outworn, we only have to imagine ourselves living in a society in which this ideal has totally faded. Values of self-aggrandisement, selfishness, survival, power and greed instead become the norm. Those too weak, too poor or too disadvantaged cannot compete in the human jungle. Who will serve them? Some might well argue that we have already created this world. Currently, the marketplace offers no morality except that of the right price and the short term. The cult of individuality has been raised to a fine art. Service implies an awareness of others.

Opening the heart does not come from being clever but from simplicity. It does not come from being knowledgeable but from being wise. It does not come from being full of self but from being empty of self. How difficult it is to live with an open heart in a society that values the clever, the knowledgeable and the egocentric. There are many meditations on the heart and its awakening. Although the particulars may vary from tradition to tradition, the same themes are universally expressed. The heart is seen as the meeting place of the human and the divine or the universal. The chamber of the heart becomes the inner sanctuary where peace is contemplated.

Finding the seed of compassion

Without a seed there will be no plant.

Geshe Rabten, *The Treasury of Dharma*

The first move towards a more universal understanding comes as we are able to look beyond the immediate self. It is so easy to value ourselves and to always put our own needs above all else. Buddhism specifically applies a brake to this egocentric view by promoting the sentiency of all beings. This teaching asks that we value and cherish non-human forms of life from the great to the small. Such teaching has a profound and real impact in the world. It is impossible, for instance, to imagine Buddhists engaging in big game hunting. At a time of endangered species and diminishing habitats, we need a philosophy to sustain our efforts against the logic of the marketplace. Buddhism suggests that we treat all sentient beings as if they had been good mothers to us. The thought is powerful, even startling. It provides a good starting point for the development of altruism. Valuing other life encourages us to find a shared place in the greater world; we do not have to own or exploit, we merely have to learn to cooperate. As we take others into account more often, so the resulting expansion of consciousness and being opens the mind and heart. Compassion is born when the personality self gives way. Thich Naht Hanh finds a simple reverence in the most ordinary of creatures:

> *Watching a green caterpillar on a leaf, we understand the importance of the caterpillar, not just from our self-centred point of view as a human but from the penetration based on the interdependence of all things. Realizing the preciousness of all life and every being, we dare not deprive the caterpillar of its life, if some day we kill a caterpillar we will feel as if we are killing ourselves that something of ourselves dies with the caterpillar.*

We instinctively recognize the diminution that self-centredness and hard-heartedness produce. As a society we need to be able to nourish compassion in any way that we can. It is a fragile enough quality in the times in which we live. In a civilization where technology is crucial for success, there is little room for compassion. When you find the seeds of compassion in yourself then you have made a contribution to the greater whole.

Unlimited friendliness: the Metta Sutta

> *The extra smile, that extra kindness can mean so much to people. This is practice.*
>
> Ani Tenzin Palmo, *Walking on Lotus Flowers*

When were you last kind to someone? When was someone kind to you? Kindness is a simple virtue quite without pretension or expectation. It is an act of openness, simplicity and unlimited friendliness. Yet it is clear that as individuals we are not as kind to one another as we might be, otherwise this simple virtue would require no special teaching. The development of kindness is a part of Buddhist practice. The Dalai Lama has even said 'My religion is kindness'. Throughout the countries of Southeast Asia monks daily recite the *Metta Sutta*. Here is a simple expression of unlimited kindness and goodwill to others. The words are attributed to the Buddha himself:

This is the Work of those who are Skilled and Peaceful who seek the good: May they be able and upright, straight forward, of gentle speech and not proud. May they be content and easily supported, unburdened with their senses calmed. May they be wise, not arrogant and without desire for the possessions of others. May they do nothing mean or that the wise would reprove.

May all beings be happy. May they live in safety and joy. All living beings, whether weak or strong, tall or stout, medium or short, seen or unseen, near or distant, born to be born, may they all be happy.

Let no one deceive another or despise any being in any state, let none by anger or hatred wish harm to another.

As a mother watches over her child, willing to risk her own life to protect her only child, so with a boundless heart should one cherish all living beings, suffusing the whole world with unobstructed loving kindness.

Standing or walking, sitting or lying down, during all one's waking hours, may one remain mindful of this heart and this way of living that is the best in the world.

Unattached to speculations, views and sense desires, with clear vision, such a person will never be reborn in the cycles of suffering.

It is perhaps salutary to know that today as every other day, the collective heart of Buddhist Southeast Asia wishes us all well. We in turn can choose to wish others well and also show kindness to those whom we encounter. There can be little doubt that the positive force of love is the single spiritual quality that all religions are agreed about. Indeed, who could disagree with the significance given to the power of love? We ourselves need love as children and adults, as parents and grandparents. Everyone benefits from the open loving heart. We can put this simple faith into practice through the meditation of the loving heart.

The Way of the Bodhisattva

Whatever merit I may have obtained, may I become thereby the soother of every pain for all living beings. The merits which I have acquired in all my rebirths through thoughts, words and deeds, all this I am giving away without regard to myself, in order to realize the salvation of all living beings.

Vow of the Bodhisattva

It is one thing to bear others in mind as best we can as we go about our daily business and ordinary lives, it is quite another matter to make the happiness of all others the central, overriding and ultimate concern of our existence.

Here is the path of transcendent becoming. In the exchange of self for others, who can fail to see the similarity between the Way of the Bodhisattva and the Christian ideal? Carrying others is the ultimate path of the heart. This is the meaning of the Greater Vehicle, which is **Mahayana** Buddhism in contrast to the Lesser Vehicle, which is **Hinayana** Buddhism. The Greater Vehicle holds all, the Lesser Vehicle holds the individual. Such high ideals appear impossible from the perspective of the ego. The all-encompassing concerns for the self keep us pinioned to our own perceived requirements. Mahayana Buddhism offers many deep exercises and meditations to counter the voice of the small self. Both analytical meditations and meditations of concentration are used. Together, these meditations foster the birth of equanimity, create a deep understanding of our dependence on others and replace self-cherishing with the cherishing of others. Such practices give birth to the **Bodhi mind**, the awakened mind, and culminate in the supreme aspiration, which is taking responsibility for all beings. When the supreme aspiration is as natural as the breath itself, the Bodhisattva intent is born.

Through this path, we see a living tradition that places the heart at its very centre. Do not think the way of the heart can be confined to any single process. Buddhism has merely articulated a particular route that renders the process of transformation visible. The path of the heart has taken numerous incarnations. Sufi mystics know the opened heart brings ecstasy. Christian mystics find the love of God here. The living experience of the heart is what matters. The name for the experience is no more than a label. Do not think that the mystical love of the heart is somehow beyond reach. When you find your heart's desire, the heart will flower.

5

being – the creative response

Creativity is an innate human quality, it is our special response to the world. The creative impetus has no limit, our human history is that of invention, adaptation and inspired action. This spark of creativity begins in the mind as an idea or visionary possibility. When the mind is enlivened by curiosity and opened to the fullness of surroundings and situations, a totally fresh insight can arise. Famously James Watt saw the potential of steam power in a boiling kettle and penicillin came into being from a skilful observation. When the mind is dulled by mental lethargy, the creative spark fades, but moments of reflection, interaction, observation and contemplation are the creative seeds for invention, expression, discovery and wonder. These essential core components of the meditative mind are the creative driving forces of human nature. Creativity is our natural inheritance as the thinking species, homo sapiens.

The power of the creative imagination is not merely content with observing the world as it is, accepting a given reality, but is capable of creating a new reality by transforming the inner as well as the outerworld.

Lama Govinda, *Creative Meditation*

The creative mind

Children create continuously through play and imagination. They are not inhibited by self-consciousness or hampered by doubting criticism. They simply create. This openness to each new experience is not unlike the openness of the meditative mind. When we are open to each moment, we can receive and we can create. Neither the creativity of the child nor the creativity of the meditative mind gives rise to artistic endeavour that seeks public approval and acclaim. This is creativity for its own sake that seeks no further recognition. Meditation awakens the mind as a whole. As the mind is awakened it responds through creativity, which is a natural function. It is a sad fact that the creative instinct rarely survives the passage into adult life. The playful and imaginative child grows up and puts down childish things. Spontaneous creativity is lost amid adolescent angst and finally extinguished by both the burdens and distractions of adult life. Though a minority will manage to keep the creative light alive, for the majority, the time for creative expression is over. Ask yourself, in what ways do you express your own creativity? What value do you place on personal creative expression? What is preventing you from being creative? Are you just too busy in life to find a space for yourself? Do you feel that you lack creative ability?

The new technology at our disposal opens up creative possibilities and opportunities never seen before in the history of this planet. Computer technology is creative technology. Here are new tools to feed the imagination and inspire the mind. Don't hang back. Here is a brand new way of expressing yourself. Creativity can never be limited to any one form, it just springs unbounded from life itself. Every society has expressed itself through its creative endeavours. The utilitarian and the liturgical, the mundane and the sacred, the performing arts and the visual arts, works great and small, all are the outpourings of the human mind seeking to translate the human experience. The human imagination knows no limits. The imaginings of one generation so often become the reality of the next. So let us celebrate human creativity in its broadest forms and look forward with great anticipation to the new creative forms that will arise as technological creativity comes into its own.

We undervalue the creative imagination at our collective peril. It is both normal and significant. Through imagination we can stand in another's shoes. We can empathize with a stranger. We can transcend the physical limitations of time and space. We can create. We can envision and inspire. Innovation and invention take root from the imagination. Great works of the imagination come to have a reality of their own. The worlds created by Tolkein or Gene Rodenberry began only in the minds of these creators but have now become mythic landscapes shared by the many. However, the imagination does not belong solely to the world of children – it is only abandoned in favour of the intellect and to our cost. Though it is easy to think of the imagination as no more than pretence or make-believe, the imagination has a deeper significance.

The breath of inspiration

Inspiration is the very heart, the central force of all meditation. But since inspiration is a spontaneous facility, it cannot be created on command, but only induced by arousing our interest or our admiration. Thus, before we can get inspired, we must prepare the ground.

Lama Govinda, *Creative Meditation*

Inspiration remains enigmatic, even to the artist. It may come as a moment of heightened awareness, a fleeting vision, or a deep but momentary impression. The word spirit is derived from the Latin *inspirare*, which means 'to breathe'. Inspiration is as subtle and invisible as the breath. Coleridge called the imagination 'a repetition in the finite mind of the eternal act of creation of the infinite I am'. In other words he likened the personal creativity of the artist to the cosmic palette of the Creator. This may seem to be an extreme sentiment that detracts from the innate creativity of the individual. Yet biographical accounts of creative individuals often reveal that inspiration is experienced as a revelation. It feels as if something is being received, not generated. Coleridge himself wrote the epic poem 'Kubla Khan' as a result of a dream. Having fallen asleep while reading about a Mogul emperor, he awoke in receipt of a whole poem. Robert Louis Stevenson said that much of his writing was developed by 'little people' in his dreams. The German chemist F.A. Kekule attributed his breakthrough with the benzene molecule to a dream in which he saw a snake with its tail in its mouth.

It is easy to see the creativity of the great names in literature, theatre, music and the arts. It seems difficult to find this same current in our own lives. We need first to change our mindset — creativity is possible and creativity is the natural activity of the awakened mind. Lama Govinda offers wise and eloquent advice:

> *All of us could be more creative if we would think less of the doings and achievements of our mundane life, of our personalities and our ambitions — if we thought more of the hidden forces and faculties within ourselves. We make programs with our brains instead of using the ever present forces of our heart. We cheat ourselves with our coarse plans and trivial aims. We do not see what is nearest to us, we do not hear the whispering voices of our heart because of the noise of our words. Our eyes are blinded by the glaring colours of daylight. Our restless life takes away our breath, our insatiable desires make our heart palpitate and cause our blood to race through the veins. Thus we do not hear the sound of other spheres, do not see the great visions, do not feel the mysterious vibrations — and the eternal stream flows past us unto the infinite from whence it came.*

Here is a plea for the open heart and the open mind. Here is a call for moments of quiet. Here is a cry to rise above the trivial and the mundane, the personality and the immediate. Here is the prompt to look within. Here is the challenge to awaken the mind through the meditative life. Here is the opportunity to find your own creative wellspring.

Sacred art

Painting is meditation for me. As soon as I pick up the brush, there is no difference from meditation.

Okbong Sunim, *Walking on Lotus Flowers*

It is no coincidence that the great meditative traditions of the world have also become rich artistic traditions. Architecture, statuary, painting, metal work, carving, casting, brush work, weaving and much more have all become part of a sacred iconography. Every tradition has expressed its experience through art of some kind. Close to home and on a small scale we can see the impact of in-depth spiritual work upon creativity through the artistic heritage of the Golden Dawn. The Hermetic Order of Golden Dawn, which formed in 1886, took its *raison d'être* from the living current of the Western spiritual tradition and proceeded to respond to its own revelation and received wisdom. This brief flowering dug deep into Celtic, Egyptian and Hermetic symbolism. It revived ancient interests and represented the symbols of the past in a fresh guise. The symbols of the Tarot were revivified here. Sacred drama in the initiatory tradition of the ancient world was restored. In the temple the creative arts were revitalized, as colour and symbol took on a spiritual significance. Creativity flowed from the temple into the outer world through literature, scholarly works and esoteric teachings. In this brief historical moment we see the same principles that have nourished the great traditions. Flowing outwards from the spiritual centre, artistic and creative endeavours express, restate and present the moment of revelation through solid form. Unlike the great traditions, which rest upon the firm foundation of the centuries, the Golden Dawn was a seed planted in unfamiliar territory. But its legacy lives on.

There is a significant but subtle difference between secular and sacred art. The first is designed to be viewed from the outside and the second is viewed from the inside. Secular art may or may not carry a message for the viewer, whereas a deeper message is invariably embedded in spiritual art. Tibetan Buddhism offers a very particular approach to its many paintings and mandalas. The beholder enters the picture as a participant. The work of art is internally recreated by the beholder down to the last detail until it stands before inner vision. Finally, ever faithful to Buddhist teaching, the beholder reverses the creative process by dissolving the vision. Here is a concept quite outside the common Western experience of artistic enjoyment. In the Tibetan tradition it is even intended that the beholder should re-experience the vision of the artist. This relationship between the original artist, the work of art and the beholder is quite unique. It is incomprehensible in purely secular terms. When artistic expression is personal, the viewer is free to draw personal conclusions and interpretations. Sacred art expresses the universal through the particular. The beholder and the creator may touch the same vision. Such a deep relationship to a work of art is only made possible through the milieu in which it has arisen. Meditation techniques train the mind to create and dissolve images in the mind's eye. It then becomes quite natural to enter the world of a painting.

Seeing with the mind's eye

The power of forming clear cut mental images is essential to progress in meditation.

Christmas Humphreys, *Concentration and Meditation*

Imagination begins with the image-making facility of the mind, often called the mind's eye. This is a normal but underdeveloped ability. The mass bombardment of external visual images has served to dampen the active imagination and make us lazy. The imagination is a much underrated mental force. We have become so used to thinking in words instead. The writer

Henry Skolimowski clearly understands the value of the creative imagination:

The power of visualization is the power of the mind. It is a form of day-dreaming which through a strange alchemy that occurs between the mind and reality, can transform imagination into reality. How this happens is a bit of a mystery but there are many important things that we do not know, we should cherish and celebrate mystery rather than be afraid of it.

Guided meditations, which employ the power to visualize images, have become increasingly popular recently. Such meditations most often take the form of directed journeys through inner symbolic landscapes. Employing this natural function regularly awakens the active imagination and brings creativity in its wake. Childlike imagination meets adult awareness in a creative fusion of ideas and possibilities; this is the opening of the mind's eye.

How observant are you? The mind's eye is directly related to the seeing eye. If you sleepwalk through life, the mind's eye will have little to draw upon. The creative imagination, which fuels visualization, draws naturally upon memory or pure imagination. In other words images can be created within the mind from solid experience or conjured from the realms of fantasy. Asked to create moonlight over water or a tree on an autumnal day, how do you fare? When the mind's eye is open, we see everyday life with new eyes. How often do we feel that our life has become bogged down? We repeat the same routines, go through the same sequences, follow the same habits, maybe even have the same thoughts over and over again. When we are in the doldrums, we instinctively want a change of scene; we hanker after the new and the different. However, even the new will become old, the novelty will tire and the doldrums will return. Much of life is routine, humdrum and repetitive. What we need is not a change of scene but a change of inner perspective: 'Change your awareness and you live in a different world, experience a different reality'.

It is no secret that particular mind-altering drugs produce a new, if temporary, perspective. The intensity of this sudden shift in awareness often astounds; creativity occurs quite spontaneously. The world is seen through new eyes; even the most mundane and ordinary take on an extraordinary quality. The very basis of perception shifts as the narrow boundaries of the five senses are dismantled. Individuals down the ages have known of the mind-expanding properties of plants and substances. However, during the 1960s the secret of the few became the property of the masses and psychedelic art, music and youth culture rose on the back of widespread mind expansion. The perspective and perception of a generation was changed. This was a revolution in consciousness. Meditation also produces a change of perspective and perception. However, this shift of awareness is not temporary but permanent, not fleeting but stable. The meditative mind is established gently. It is built from within. The meditative mind is the creative mind. Open the inner eye, which is the eye of vision. Awaken the creative imagination by utilizing your image-making facility in the most ordinary circumstances.

The inner world: the mandala

The mandala is like a map of the world, which we want to explore and realize in the great venture which is meditation.

Lama Govinda, *Creative Meditation*

A map represents the outer world. We are familiar with its symbols. This symbolic representation enables us to journey in the outer world. The mandala is a map of the inner world. If we wish to travel in the inner world, we need to become familiar with the symbolism of the specialized map. It is a mistake to view a mandala purely as a work of art; it is a piece of sacred art with a specific intent. The mandala has been described as 'a geometric projection of the world reduced to an essential pattern'. Although mandalas have evolved within different traditions, the same principle applies. Art expresses a precise and particular symbolic language, which has been codified through centuries of meditative experience. Images and symbols resonate with the vocabulary of the psyche; words alone do not touch these deeper levels of being. This is the essential difference between the sacred and the mundane. Sacred art is never idiosyncratic but universal, never random but precise. It appeals not to the senses but to the soul, not to the eye but to the awakened mind.

In the specialized language of the sacred, every detail of colour and composition has a place and purpose. The mandala takes the circle as its form and may contain further concentric circles. The central point has special significance; lines radiate from this point and cut the circle into four cardinal segments. A square commonly surrounds the central point, creating further triangular areas. The basic geometric forms of circle, square and triangle are endlessly elaborated. Within the area of the mandala, the four cardinal directions are often marked with gates. The architectural images lend themselves naturally to an inner landscape. The different areas take on symbolic scenic qualities, such as gardens in paradise, courtyards and chambers. The mandala becomes a palace or a representation of the ideal city where the individual undertakes a journey to the centre.

The ability to enter the realm of the mandala clearly depends upon the ability to bring it to life in the mind. The structure of the mandala is fixed in the mind before the meditation proceeds. To the observer the mandala remains no more than a two-dimensional image. To the active participant the mandala becomes an inner world that comes to life through meditation. In Tantric Buddhism the mandala is approached through the East, the place of sunrise. The journey through the inner landscape follows the prescribed route to the centre, which is both the human heart and the axis of the universe. The mandala is the universal temple on top of the sacred mountain. Jung rediscovered the significance of the mandala form for himself. He wrote, 'Only gradually did I discover what the mandala really is. Formation, Transformation, Eternal Mind's eternal recreation.'

6

doing – the way of activity

Although meditation is often viewed as a seated and silent activity of private focus, this same point of focus can be transferred to all activities, making meditation active and dynamic. The components of the meditative mind: focus, awareness, concentration and realization, are the same mental skills needed to achieve success in all areas of life: sports, martial arts, music, dance and all physically or psychologically challenging situations. It is perhaps not coincidental that today coaching for excellence embraces many of the same techniques employed in meditation. Sharp mental focus is always visible in great performance. New applications for the meditative mind are currently appearing in the newly emerging synthesis between Eastern techniques and Western needs. This new impetus has the potential to reshape the way we learn and apply the mind. So take meditative focus into the active and physical aspects of your life where mental preparation will enhance the outcome.

Trivial participation ultimately bores you, leaves behind a sense of shallowness, contributes little to your deeper sense of life. Significant participation, on the other hand, engages you, enthrals and satisfies you, it contributes to the meaning of your life.

Henry Skolimowski, *EcoYoga*

The integrated life

Once the meditative mind has been established, it is not confined to a particular posture or place. Rather the meditative mind is continuously present. It will suffuse mundane activities and transform the everyday into meditative practice. In the words of Ani Tenzin Palmo, 'Practice is something you do moment to moment, all through the day. It is the way you relate to the people you meet. It is the way you drink your tea, approach your work and how you become more aware of your internal responses to things.' When the so-called mundane and the so-called spiritual merge into a seamless garment, there is just the One Life sanctified and made meaningful. Our difficulty in reconciling the spiritual with the material reflects the deep split that still exists in Western philosophy. Only holistic philosophy finds no gap between these two poles; holistic philosophy upholds the integration of opposites and affirms interconnectedness.

Ecological spirituality

What the universe is depends on you; treat it like a machine and it becomes a machine; treat it like a divine place and it becomes a divine place.

Henry Skolimowski, *EcoYoga*

The Way of Activity is the natural complement to the Way of Contemplation. Activity is the extension of awareness, an expression of choice and a statement of clear motivation. In this way, life takes on a single focus and sharp direction through word and deed, thought and action. The inner life cannot be separated from its outer expression. When we have experienced a deep connection to others and the greater world, it is impossible to deny this truth. Once we have seen the invisible threads that bind everything together it is impossible to act as an isolated being. Changes in consciousness bring changes in action. Meditation brings an expansion of consciousness. As consciousness expands we become aware of the greater currents at work in the world today. Once we have awoken to ecological spirituality we can only accept the responsibilities that understanding brings. We have no option but to act accordingly.

Henry Skolimowski holds the chair of Ecological Philosophy at the University of Warsaw in Poland. He is the founder of Eco-Philosophy, a practical, spiritual, holistic philosophy that addresses the needs of our times. Like many other spiritual voices of today, he calls for participation in the world, not escape from it. In his book, *EcoYoga*, he takes Yoga into a new arena. He envisages the world as a sanctuary to be approached with reverence. He reminds us that this idea is itself empowering, so take the image into daily life and discover what your role is in the sanctuary of the world. He offers meditations that are experienced through life itself. His meditations are those that bring us into closer contact with the landscape, with trees, rocks and running water. He reminds us to walk in beauty. He urges us to realize our own potential. He asks us to remember the main focus of EcoYoga – grace, health and hope. The meditations he offers are simple and gentle, life affirming and reverential. He too gives us integrated meditation, spiritual thought and dynamic action. Skolimowski writes: 'A deep comprehension of ecology is reverence in action. This reverence is a form of spirituality. In our times the ecological and the spiritual become one. This is the foundation of ecological spirituality.' He continues, 'Healing the planet and ourselves is spiritual work of the first magnitude in our day and age. Who can deny the truth of this statement? Whatever may be our race and religion, ecology binds us all together. Ecology is the universal religious project of our times.' Here is the way of activity that beckons us all. It was the Greeks who called the earth

Gaia. This name has become a rallying call for all who love the world, so in your meditation call her name too.

Ecological spirituality has a real significance and meaning. This is no esoteric byway but a broad and rewarding path. The issues that face the world at this time are global. Ecology knows no national boundaries. Gaia is the world itself. This is a much needed universal image for a common humanity. Your meditations upon Gaia will lead you into a unique relationship. Earth wisdom comes to those who live close to nature but industrialization has rendered us proud and forgetful. Skolimowski acknowledges the significance of this newly remembered spiritual path: 'Thus a new religion is emerging, the religion which follows from the yoga of reverence for Mother Earth. Its church is the entire Cosmos.' Here is the way of activity, which is relevant for today and tomorrow.

The cosmic dance

The dance opens a door in the soul to divine influences.

Sultan Walad

People have danced together since the earliest times. The imprints of stamping feet have been found in Neolithic caves when dance probably brought the group together in celebration, triumph or sorrow. Movement is intimately connected with human emotion. Dance naturally lends itself to deep expression – the body speaks in movement, the steps speak through rhythm and sequence. Here is a universal non-verbal language that speaks through the eloquence of shared symbol. Dance is an ancient sacred form. In ancient Egypt, Hathor was the goddess of music and dance. Her priestesses performed sacred dance to evoke the presence of divine beauty and harmony. The sacred dance was able to take participants and worshippers into states of ecstatic bliss. In India, temple dancers portrayed the stories of the deities in movement and gesture. In Bali, dance was offered in the temple. The great traditions of sacred dance have been eclipsed. We are left with the desire to reconnect, to revitalize and renew, for the spirit of the dance never dies.

In the infancy of the twentieth century the free-spirited Isadora Duncan reinterpreted movement during a time of oppressive materialism and formality; her dancing was radical. She found inspiration in the classical past of Greece and danced barefoot in simple flowing garments. She expressed the liberation of the human spirit through spontaneous and graceful movement. She was unique; with her passing this exuberant but all too brief flirtation with dance of the spirit was over. Her life revitalized the sacred dance once again. She gave others the courage to share in the dance of life. As the twentieth century unfolded others again looked to the spiritual dimensions of dance. Rudolph Steiner, whose spiritual vision encompassed every aspect of the mundane life from organic farming to education, also saw the spiritual in dance. He created a new approach to movement, which he called Eurythmy. This combined movement and gesture in synchronous harmony with the spoken word. Accordingly every consonant corresponds to a movement. The movements of Eurythmy are soft and flowing, gentle and expressive. He wrote, 'Man is a form proceeding out of movement. Eurythmy is a continuation of divine movement, of the divine form in man. By means of Eurythmy man approaches nearer to the divine.'

More recently still there has been a revival of circle dancing as spiritual expression. The circle is a natural symbol. The circular dance easily becomes the cycle of the year, the girdle of the zodiac, or simply the gathering of the clan. As we dance in the circle, we also tread the magic circle and create a shared sacred space. As the circle naturally expresses human interaction and understanding, so spinning or whirling also seems to be a natural movement. Children often spin and whirl in playground games until giddiness and laughter take over. Since the earth spins on its axis, spinning too is a symbolic movement. The Sufi Master Jaluddin Rumi founded the Mevlevi Order which is more commonly known as the Order of Whirling Dervishes. The whirling dance is a moving meditation. The dancer undertakes a series of inner images which bind the cosmic to the mundane, the individual to creation. The dance expresses the unity of life, through the unity of thought and action. The right hand of the dancer is upturned to receive divine blessing. The left hand points down to transmit the living presence to the world. Curiously, this dance was banned, though now special permits are given to perform it for tourists; the sacred is secularized and put up for sale.

The allegorical garden

It is a spot beyond imagination
Delighted to the heart, where roses bloom,
And sparkling fountains murmur – where the earth
Is rich with many-coloured flowers; and musk
Floats on the gentle breezes, hyacinths
And lilies add their perfume – golden fruits
Weigh down the branches of the lofty trees.

Firdawsi

What does your garden mean to you? Is it a place of delight or a place of drudgery? Is it heaven on earth or hell on earth? Whatever your garden is for you, to the Persians the garden represented an image of paradise. It provided the physical opportunity to create an image of the celestial. The gardens of Paradise are described in the Qur'an (55: 45–75). The four gardens within the Paradise Garden are the Garden of the Soul, the Garden of the Heart, the Garden of the Spirit and the Garden of the Essence. These are the four stages through which the mystic travels. This description has inspired a long lived and beautiful tradition of the garden as spiritual allegory. Here is a way of activity that literally combines the spiritual and the earthly: as virgin soil is landscaped, it is redesigned in the image of the divine through proportion, arrangement, metaphor and living symbol.

Water was a constant theme in the form of pools, lakes, channels and fountains. More than merely forming a beautiful sight in the garden, water represented the spiritual light. As a fountain the spiritual light nourished and fed the whole garden. It imparted a full flavour to the many fruits. Plums, cherries, quinces, lemons, apricots, mulberries, figs, oranges, limes, pomegranates and grapes were a luscious harvest, but such fruits also represented thoughts nurtured on the Tree of Life. Water was admired at its surface for its reflective sheen as a mirror of passing reality. The surface was at times decorated with strewn rose petals or beautified by lilies in bloom. Open water channels were lined with blue tiles to deepen the reception of colour and the sound of splashing water was enhanced by changes of level to awaken perception. Every detail was important in this living symbolic landscape. The depths of the larger pools symbolized the dark and unfathomable mystery of life itself. The Persian garden was lit by many flowers but most favoured was the rose. This was already rich with symbolic and mystical connotation from spiritual poetry where the beloved, the soul, was identified with the rose. Trees were planted in abundance as symbols of life and immortality.

Here is an activity that you can make your own. Symbolic planting and colour can be brought to life in the simplest garden. Spiritual ideas and themes can be represented in ways of your own choosing. Let your creativity and spiritual inspiration live. The garden lives too. Here is a place for both contemplative meditation and active meditation. Here is where you can meet Gaia through the round of the seasons. If you love the engagement of the gardening process from seed to plant, you have many opportunities to interact with the living energies of nature. Here is a way of participation – be inventive, be creative. The garden lives, it reveals the interdependence of all things. Let head, heart and hands be united through a single expression and join the way of activity.

Sacred shrines

The act of creating sacred space recapitulates the stages of creation.

Patee Kryder, *Sacred Ground to Sacred Space*

As meditation creates changes in consciousness, so aspirations, goals and intentions change too. We become more discriminating and more focused on what is important to us. As this process gathers momentum, it becomes quite natural to represent these areas through symbol and image. We join the ancient and universal tradition of shrinemakers and keepers. Here too is a way of activity as we select items of importance and colours of significance to express our spiritual presence. Shrine building begins with a simple question: what is sacred to you? Answering the question not in words but representations takes us towards the building of a personal shrine. This can be very simple. It need be no more than a small space on a shelf or table top. It does not even need to draw attention to itself; an arrangement of flowers, stones or shells with a small candle is as eloquent as anything large and ornate. The shrine merely represents the fact that you choose outwardly to recognize what you inwardly acknowledge to be sacred. The items will change as you change.

The family shrine or household shrine is very common in the East but rather uncommon in the West where state-based religion and communal worship has dominated. Creating a shrine as a focal point for your spiritual life is a creative affirmation of your spiritual intent. Shrine building will put you in touch with the great artistic and cultural traditions of the world for which civilization has not built shrines. If you follow this impetus, you will encounter archetypal forms in numerous historical guises. You will discover the inner significance of geometry, sacred architecture and colour. You will find the sacred symbols of peoples past and present but most of all you will find what is sacred to you. Here is the place for the beautiful and the natural, the painted and the crafted, the constructed and the found. Here is the place for the sacred in your home and heart.

The difference between thinking and doing is substantial. The mind creates rapidly and without limitation. Images can be conjured from the imagination or from memory. Mental images enjoy no permanent form and remain invisible to all but the creator.

When a vision is translated into physical form it becomes tangible and accessible. The shrine encapsulates feeling and intent, aspiration and devotion, which transcend the purely intellectual mind. Sacred images serve as a focus for further meditation, which gives rise to new insight and inspiration in a dynamic and continuous relationship.

7

changing – the flow of life

We are living through a period of unprecedented change; rapid change can be unsettling as the opposing forces of resistance and propulsion are at work. The old and the new jostle against each other uncomfortably. Like the classic yin-yang symbol of dark and light, change and constancy are inseparably united and part of a greater whole. Even though it is only natural to cling to the known and the secure, change is inevitable. Progress through life is a passage of change from birth to death. Embracing the future and releasing the past asks for openness of both heart and mind, permitting the unknown to take seed as the possible, and a transparency of being, which enables the past to be dissolved and makes space for growth and renewal. Contemplating the impermanence of all things is a salutary reminder that nothing can hold back the flow of time and change.

Time and tide wait for no man.

Time and tide

The fabric of our ordinary lives appears so regular, so predictable, sometimes even stagnant. It is easy to see the life of home and work, commitment and responsibility as a permanent fixture. This is always illusory. Within routine, change is constant. Nothing is permanent; this is the flow of life. It is the Demon Impermanence who holds the Wheel of Life in his clutches; he has us all in his grip, whether we know it or not. Recognizing the impermanence of all things is a powerful realization. The news of a life-threatening illness can shake us to the core; it brings us face to face with our own impermanence. So often such news serves to galvanize intentions and focus motivations. Priorities shift instantly and we suddenly see what is really important with devastating clarity. Such shocks put life in perspective. But it need not take a tragedy to remind us of the obvious. We can keep our priorities in focus through choice and awareness. We cannot hide in the delusion of permanence. We cannot halt the passing of time. We cannot control the flow of life, but we can flow with it.

Contemporary Western society is organized by the clock and the timetable, the meeting and the schedule, the diary and the planner. Being on time is a virtue, being late is unforgivable. This continual deference to the clock is highly stressful and places daily life within shared constraints. While it seems impossible to escape the obligations of timekeeping in the outer world, we might benefit by keeping this in balance with an inner sense of time. Yet Nature has her own rhythms too. Sunrise and sunset are the twin poles of the natural day. There is something wonderfully magical as the sun appears over the horizon and the day breaks. The moment of sunset is equally wonderful as the sun sinks and darkness spreads. These are Nature's markers, the continual play of change

64   find peace with meditation

and interdependency. Have you watched the sun rise? Have you watched the sun set?

Sunrise and sunset have a reality which transcends the clock and the timekeeping devices of our own world. As we watch the moment of sunrise, we can reflect upon the countless generations who have done the same. As we watch daybreak we can know that civilizations now long dead also observed the same event. Who has not seen the sun rise and set? Peoples unknown and unnamed, peoples forgotten in memory and distant in time have lived by the moments of dawn and dusk. The sun opens and closes for all: Buddhists and Hindus, Sikhs and Sufis, Christians and Muslims alike. Watching the coming and going of day and night puts us in touch with the flow of life which is change. Take sunrise and sunset as your meditations and let nature be your teacher.

The sun has much to teach the observant watcher for it marks out seasonal rhythms too: the place of sunrise and sunset on the horizon move as the year progresses. This apparently moving light traces out a seasonal dance. We no longer live upon the empty horizon; we have forgotten the dance of the sun. Midsummer and midwinter are the twin poles of the solar year, so why not make the effort to become conscious of this fundamental pattern. The sun on the horizon keeps us in touch with the flow of life. These seasonal solstice landmarks hold the cycle of the year. These are the natural cycles, which cannot be denied, moved or mistaken. The cycle of the natural year has become swamped by the demands we place on ourselves. Less technological societies have taken these seasonal landmarks as the basis for spiritual celebration and festivity. As the wheel of the year turns, so we turn too. As we internalize this natural movement, we begin to realize that all is moving, the earth turns constantly on its own axis and also takes up its own orbit through space. The moon dances around the earth too. Nothing is still. The cosmic dance is an ancient image for the interplay of creation and we forget the dance only at our own cost.

When we replace the cosmic dance with a frozen, hard-edged reality, we compartmentalize life into things separated by insurmountable boundaries. We may not realize it, but we have already taken a step towards freezing the movement of the life we live. Realizing the interdependence of all existence prevents us from committing this fatal flaw. We see interdependence in every way in every day, though we often remain unconscious of it. We see it at every level of life from the cosmic to the mundane. It is demonstrated for us continuously and totally. All we need to do is become aware of this great interdependent web that holds us all. The phenomena that define the shape of our lives are all interdependent pieces of a vast jigsaw of being, day and night, sunrise and sunset, solstice and equinox. Dawn and dusk, sunlight and moonlight each exist in relationship, not as separate objects. The relationship between sun and moon shows us an interdependent relationship that we so often take for granted. The moon has no light of its own but reflects the light of the sun to us, which we see in a cyclic pattern of light and dark. The moon is full when it is opposite the light of the sun and it is dark when it receives no light from the sun. Its growing and diminishing, the waxing and waning of the moon, are statements of relationship. The lunar cycle of 29½ days is a statement of interdependence. Watch the moon and take interdependence as your theme; once you have begun to see the interdependence of all life, you will understand that this is the web that supports your existence and you will move a step closer to the flow of life.

Flowing with daily life

Each thought, each action in the sunlight of awareness becomes sacred. In this light, no boundaries exist between the sacred and the profane.

Thich Nhat Hanh, *The Sun My Heart*

Once again we are indebted to the simple wisdom of Thich Nhat Hanh for the endearing book *Present Moment, Wonderful*

Moment. His philosophy is so straightforward: if you live fully in every moment, you will live fully. Who can find fault with this? Meditation takes place from the foundations of everyday life. It develops and flowers within everyday life. Meditation is intimately and wholly related to everyday life and in turn everyday life is changed through meditation. For a moment stand back from the requirements of your everyday life – look at it with a detached eye. How do you go about the daily round? Do you engage with daily life or do you want every day to be over as quickly as possible? Does your daily life appear to be dull and monotonous? Are you awake in life or do you sleepwalk from one day to the next? Thich Nhat Hanh asks us, 'How many days slip by in forgetfulness? What are you doing with your life?'

Lama Govinda also addresses the way in which we perceive daily life: 'Habit kills intuition, because habit prevents living experience, direct perception.' What have you done today? Where have you been today? What will you do tomorrow? Is your life governed by routine, habit and predictability? Don't be afraid to admit that it is, because routine, regularity and predictability form a big and important part of life. It is not regularity of lifestyle, but habitual thinking that destroys. Monastic life is orderly and disciplined. Paradoxically, it is the life of habit that gives freedom. What did you notice today? What did you notice about today or did it appear just like any other day to you? Does every day appear to be the same? Even a moment's clear reflection will show you that every day cannot be the same as another. What did you notice on your way to work? What were you aware of at work today? What did you notice at home today? Tomorrow, be conscious of the opportunity, become aware and you will find something new in tomorrow. Take meditation into your ordinary daily life. Take it with you when you walk or shop or visit a friend. Meditation is not confined to sitting in a meditation posture. It may begin in this way but it will in time expand into ordinary life. It becomes a way of looking at life, a way of seeing with open eyes. When your eyes are open, you will walk in the flow of life and be responsive to it.

Being here and now

When I eat, I eat; when I sleep, I sleep.

Traditional Zen saying

So much of life is bound up with relationships, family and friends. Few are the folk who choose to give up this base in favour of the monastic life. Family life with all its normal ups and downs is the place where mindfulness can serve us well. Running a home and bringing up a family is continually demanding. Mindfulness is ever required in relationships if we are to interact with sensitivity and understanding. It could be argued that it is within family life and ordinary circumstances that mindfulness practice is tested to capacity. How many busy mothers would not cheerfully choose a monastic retreat – just briefly of course – perhaps until the regular ritual of children's bedtime has passed anyway! In many ways mindfulness is an extension of the loving care given by parents in the normal course of life. Christine Feldman, mother of two and co-founder of a meditation retreat centre in Devon, affirms what every parent knows: 'Parenting challenges you at every level of your being. All the things that are important in meditation practice – patience, forgiveness, letting go, compassion, steadfastness and equanimity – are the things that are also important in parenting. Children provide opportunities to develop, nurture and nourish these qualities in direct and dynamic ways.' A parent seeks to be aware of a child's needs, even the unspoken ones, to listen to what is said both in word and intent, to understand developmental needs and to be responsive and loving. If such needs were mindlessly ignored, only unhappiness would follow. So mindfulness does not have to be treated as an esoteric or arcane discipline; you are already mindful.

Spiritual aspiration is often symbolized by an arrow in flight. The arrow is loosed into the future; it lands like a marker for us. Reflect on those qualities that will support your future practice and those qualities that will not. To clarify your ideas make a list. It is likely that qualities such as patience, kindness, simplicity, trust and forgiveness will be among your list of supporting qualities. On the other hand, anger, fear, intolerance, laziness and impatience will probably be on your list of non-supportive qualities. Spend some time making your list. When it is complete, look at yourself and honestly evaluate the way in which these qualities function within you. Decide which qualities you need to develop and which need to be diminished. When you have come to a decision, be prepared to use daily life as the opportunity to create change. Daily life presents us with continuous choices; to be kind or unkind, thoughtful or thoughtless, patient or impatient. Observe yourself. Particular situations probably create the same reactions over and over. As soon as we see the pattern, we are in a position to intervene and consciously react differently. This kind of self-observation is not unique to Buddhism. Rabbi Nachman, a founder of the Hasidic movement, stressed the importance of taking stock regularly: 'You must therefore make sure to set aside a specific time each day to calmly review your life.'

Impermanence: the teacher

You don't know what you've got till it's gone.

Joni Mitchell

The words of the song ring horribly true for all of us. How many times have we wished to put the clock back or to be given a second chance? But time moves on relentlessly and second chances are few and far between. How often do we regret the things said or unsaid, the unfinished business, the unresolved issues that we leave in our wake? Buddhists believe that here lies the fuel of our future karma. Here are seeds waiting to come to fruition in the future. Whether we believe in the power of unfinished business to draw us back into future incarnations or not, we can still recognize unfinished business in ourselves. It is easy to live in pretence. It often seems preferable to truth. The truth is that human life is limited and we have an impermanent form in an ever changing world. Change and impermanence are frightening, for we most often seek security and stability. When we only remember security and forget impermanence, we have missed the fundamental paradox of being alive. When we remember paradox, we look towards truth. Impermanence is the last thing we wish to face.

How reticent we are to talk about death, the last taboo. How reticent we are, even to think about death. Death remains the greatest fear of all. Our fear is not diminished by ignoring this reality. Who feels comfortable thinking about their own death? Who is willing to take personal death as a subject for meditation? Yet besides birth, death is perhaps the only other certainty. And yet this is our greatest fear. It holds the terror of the unknown and the call of the inevitable. Rather than face this certain destiny, we choose to ignore this reality until the very moment when death comes calling. Until we face death, we are not free to find life. Spiritual traditions universally offer meditations on death. The Sufis say 'die before you die'. Osho's words too have an immediacy:

> *Start meditating on death. And whenever you feel death close by, go into it through the door of love, through the door of meditation, through the door of a man dying. And if some day you are dying – and the day is going to come one day – receive it in joy, benediction. And if you can receive death in joy and benediction, you will attain to the greatest peak, because death is the crescendo of life.*

Osho died on 19 January 1990.

If we seek life, we too must face the reality of death as all the previous generations of spiritual travellers have done. Our fears will not be unique and our worries will not be personal, but a restatement of all the human fears and concerns down the ages. Buddhism asks that we address the subject of death. It offers graduated meditations that bring us face to face with the concept of death through small steps. The first step is to reflect that death is inevitable. We need to think about the fact that everybody is going to die and that there is no place we can go to avoid death.

Second, we are asked to reflect on the fact that the time of death is uncertain. We do not have a fixed lifespan. We do not know when death will come. Small things can cause our death and there is no guarantee of a long life. Third, we are asked to envisage the close of life and ponder upon what has been worthwhile. These three stages help us find what is really important in our lives.

8

hearing – the power of sound

Meeting sacred sound opens a new avenue of experience and exploration: the chant, the mantra, devotional music, song and the naked voice offer a dynamic spiritual vocabulary; sound can become meditation. This practical encounter brings a new perspective to everyday living and enhances our experience of the world as a place of living vibrations. Entering into a relationship with sacred sound brings creativity and healing, as a receptive space opens in the deeper mind. It is common to view meditation as a passive mental activity, but meditating through the application of sound adds a new active dimension of experience. Incorporating sounded meditation into your practice additionally brings enlivening mental, physical and psychological benefits as well as a sense of spiritual communion. Expressing the spiritual through mind, heart and voice together brings a profound sense of unity and common humanity which uplifts and enhances life. Encountering the special qualities of sacred sound can prove to be a life-changing moment, the rediscovery of the forgotten legacy can become a new adventure on the path of personal change and transformation.

The origin of healing by sound and music can be traced into prehistory and beyond, into the realms of myth, religion and the memory of the soul.

Olivia Dewhurst Maddock, *The Book of Sound Therapy*

The sound of silence

Television, radio, personal CD players and stereo systems, in-car sound systems, in-store music and wrap-around sound all contribute to a sound-filled experience. This is the environment we now take for granted. Technology brings instant sound to the home, the workplace and the car. This is mundane sound which is the voice of the world at work.

Where is silence now as you read these words? What sounds can you hear at this moment? Stop and become attuned to them. What do you hear? Where is silence for you? When did you last sit in silence? Perhaps the very word reminds you of the enforced silence in the library or the schoolroom. Yet silence need not be oppressive or uncomfortable. Silence is a powerful symbol for the qualities of emptiness and spaciousness, which we seek through meditation. The empty mind is the open mind; the spacious mind is the free mind. The silent moment is empty and spacious. Do you have any moments of silence in your life? Reflect for a moment upon the many different sounds that punctuate our lives: alarm calls, phone calls, radio and television in the home, piped music in shops, stereo sound in cars, traffic on the streets, machinery in the factory, technology in the office. Where is silence?

If we want silence we will need consciously to create it. How often do we turn on the radio or even the television 'just for company'? This is not conscious listening but unconscious listening. We fill the empty space with the noise of the human voice. We pay no attention to what is being said, we are simply happy with the sound of company. When an opportunity presents itself, you will be able to choose between sound and silence. What will you choose? Seek out a silent space, create a silent space and savour it. Silence teaches us how to value sound and sound teaches us how to value silence.

Listening

The Yoga of listening is controlling your ego so that it does not only hear what it wants to hear.

Henry Skolimowski, *EcoYoga*

Listening is not the same as hearing. It is easy to hear without listening. Hearing is passive but listening is active. Listening is a skill. When we listen to something, whether a person or a piece of music, we give our active attention so that we listen for meaning. The human voice reveals as much through intonation and emphasis as through words. The subtle nuances that convey well-being or frustration, confidence or fear, contentment or anxiety, are to be found in sound rather than words. Politeness and social conformity easily mask what is really being said. A good listener will hear the meaning through the words and will relate to intent rather than content. True communication lies in listening not just hearing.

The sounds of Nature

May all embodied creatures
Uninterruptedly hear
The sound of Dharma issuing from birds and trees,
Beams of light and even space itself.

From *The Shantiveda*

The sounds of technology have obscured the sounds of Nature. The sounds of technology cannot heal. There is no comfort in mechanical clatter, in electrical chatter or in the tapping of the keyboard. These are the sounds of work, the voice of commerce and the world of the marketplace. There is no healing for the soul here. Yet these are the sounds we value; these are the status symbols of our success. Now imagine for a moment the sound of waves pouring onto a shingle beach. Can you hear the rasp as wave and beach embrace briefly? Can you hear the flutter of stones being carried and turned? Can you hear the crash as a deeper wave drops onto water before rushing towards the shore? These sounds are deeply ingrained within us, whether from the memory of childhood or even some deeper ancestral memory; we respond to this ancient and primordial sound of Nature. Not only does this sound relax and soothe but it seems to strip away the veneer of modernity in an instant. We are touched by a deeper current, for the waves broke upon the beach long before our most distant ancestors stood and heard the same sound. Nature has many sounds but unless we make an effort to hear them, we will remain in the prison house of the technological and the industrial. When did you last hear water trickling over stone, leaves rustling in the breeze or bird song? Hearing these sounds in the memory or imagination whets the appetite for the real encounter, so open your inner ear to Nature's many voices.

Creative sound

You live in a world of sounds. Sounds heard and unheard; sounds musical and chaotic; sounds strange and familiar; sounds stressful and pleasing; sounds that shatter and sounds that heal.

Olivia Dewhurst-Maddock, *Sound as Therapy*

The often quoted work by Ernst Chladni provides a fascinating insight into the relationship between sound and form. Chladni observed a clear relationship between vibration and pattern. In his experiments, sand sprinkled onto metal plates reacted to the different notes of a violin bow. As the bow was stroked against the plate consistent patterns appeared. These plates and their patterns have subsequently been called Chladni disks. His work was followed by others, notably Hans Jenny, who developed methods that permitted greater accuracy and measurement. Jenny found that electrical impulses upon crystal lattices provided precise measurement. He experimented with different substances including liquids, dyes, glycerine, powders and gels. Every medium produced patterns in response to vibration. Movement began, pattern took shape, and then symmetry appeared. Metamorphosis was constant as tone and note were varied. Increased pitch created complexity. Delicate patterns appeared on films of water in response to vibration. Regular lattice formations appeared in sheets of glycerine. His increasingly sophisticated experiments with metal plates and piezoelectric vibrations reveal mandala-like images, which contained a central point with circular forms.

With the creation of a new instrument, which Jenny called the tonoscope, these experiments were extended to observe the effect of the human voice. An electrostatic variant even translated music into form, making it possible to see the music of Mozart and watch the sonatas of Bach in continuous motion.

The sounded word

Om Mane Padme Hum.

Tibetan Mantra

The fascinating work of cymatics bridges sound and form. It renders the invisible visible. It shows us what we hear. It takes us directly into the tradition of the word as sounded meditation. Sounded words or phrases are currently known as *mantras*. There are mantras of many kinds from simple syllables, to words and meaningful phrases. Each functions at more than one level simultaneously. It is possible to translate mantra but this only provides an intellectual understanding. The mantra is more than this as the tonoscope has so clearly revealed to us. Something beyond our rational comprehension takes place as the mantra is sounded. It has long been maintained that one of the secrets of the mantra lies in its correct sounding. This is given between teacher and pupil; it cannot be learned from the printed word. The tonoscope supports this. Not only do we see the vibrating effect of vowels taking visible shape but in a staggering demonstration of an ancient truth, the mantra *OM* when correctly sounded produces the *Shri yantra* as its visible counterpart. The universal mantra, the sound of the eternal, produces cosmic creation.

9

waking – the enlightenment breakthrough

The idea of enlightenment is both fascinating and puzzling since it suggests that we normally live in an unenlightened state. Throughout history, individuals have experienced a sudden glimpse into a greater life, as if a curtain had suddenly been drawn back revealing a previously unseen stage. This new perspective does not create estranged or alienated people but wholly normal and full human beings. Enlightenment is perhaps the crowning human experience.

Those best qualified to share the moment of revelation have also been those most reluctant to discuss it; personal description would be converted into the bedrock of hard truth by the unenlightened. There remain relatively few accounts to which we can turn as reference points. Nevertheless, this experience belongs to all traditions and times, to all peoples and places.

*Let me show how far our nature is enlightened or
unenlightened.*

Plato, *Book VII*

Waking up

Many spiritual stories are about waking up. The verb *buddha*
means to wake up. One who wakes up is called a *Buddha*. It is
difficult to accept the idea that we sleepwalk through life's many
circumstances, yet it is a universal and age-old idea.

In the tradition of the spirituality awakened, Osho writes,
'You are fast asleep, and you don't know who you are.' How difficult
it is to recall the details of ordinary waking life through the filter of
ordinary consciousness. Do you remember the conversations that
you have undertaken in the past with friends, family, colleagues
and opponents? How many special moments in your life do you
remember? How many ordinary times can you recall? What were
you thinking about yesterday mid-morning? What was the nature
of your life aspiration a year ago?

The graduated path to enlightenment might be thought of
as a conscious system for destructuring the perception system:
'The complexity of the brain tends to insulate us from the reality
of pure consciousness surrounding us. As all meditation systems
seem to concur, we "tune in" to pure consciousness by stilling the
fruits of the brain's complexity.' This conscious weakening of the
internal model permits us to perceive directly without the screen of
the inner conceptual world. The moment of enlightenment is most
often experienced as a radical breakthrough, as if we see the world
for the very first time. 'An experience which is not yet limited by
preconceived ideas has all the qualities of infinity.' (Brian Lancaster)

Enlightenment: the inner light

*Every individual has the potentiality to become enlightened
in the course of this life or later existences.*

Lama Govinda, *Creative Meditation*

Light is often used as a metaphor for spiritual awakening. It serves well as a symbol for clarity and understanding. Sudden moments of great clarity are more than metaphorical and such breakthrough moments take place in reality as a matter of daily life. Sometimes these breakthroughs assume cataclysmic proportions and seem to shatter and simultaneously reshape our view of reality.

The experience of enlightenment is not confined to the great and famous mystics of history. This is a living reality that the ordinary person can also touch in the world of today. The story rendered by a Canadian housewife is especially interesting. After seven days of intense inner labour and spiritual incubation, she experienced her first enlightenment:

The days and weeks that followed were the most deeply happy and serene of my life. There was no such thing as a 'problem'. Past relationships to people who had once caused me deep disturbance I now saw with perfect understanding. For the first time in my life I was able to move like the air, in any direction, free at last from the self which had always been such a tormenting bond to me.

Some six years later she experienced a second awakening:

One spring day as I was working in the garden, the air seemed to shiver in a strange way, as though the usual sequence of time had opened into a new dimension, and I became aware that something untoward was about to happen, if not that day then soon. Hoping to prepare in some way for it, I doubled my regular sittings of Zazen and studied Buddhist books late into each night.

A few evenings later, after carefully sifting through The Tibetan Book of the Dead *and then taking my bath, I sat in front of a painting of the Buddha and listened quietly by candlelight to a slow movement of Beethoven's A Minor Quartet, a deep expression of man's self-renunciation, and then went to bed. The next morning, just after breakfast, I suddenly felt as though I were being struck by a bolt of lightning, and I began to tremble. All at once the whole trauma of my difficult birth flashed into my mind. Like a key, this opened dark rooms of secret resentments and hidden fears which flowed out of me like poisons. Tears gushed out and so weakened me I had to lie down. Yet a deep happiness was there. ... Slowly my focus changed:*

'I'm dead! There's nothing to call me. There never was a me! It's an allegory, a mental image, a pattern upon which nothing was ever modelled.' I grew dizzy with delight. Solid objects appeared as shadows, and everything my eyes fell upon was radiantly beautiful. These words can only hint at what was revealed to me in the days that followed.

1 *The world as apprehended by the senses is the least true (in the sense of complete), the least dynamic (in the sense of eternal movement), and the least important in a vast 'geometry of existence' of unspeakable profundity, whose rate of vibration, whose intensity and subtlety are beyond verbal description.*

2 *Words are cumbersome and primitive – almost useless in trying to suggest the true multi-dimensional workings of an indescribably vast complex of dynamic force, to contact which one must abandon one's normal level of consciousness.*

3 *The least act, such as eating or scratching an arm, is not at all simple. It is merely the visible movement in a network of causes and effects reaching forward into Unknowingness and back into an infinity of Silence where individual consciousness cannot even enter. There is truly nothing to know, nothing that can be known.*

4 *The physical world is an infinity of movement, of Time-Existence. But simultaneously it is an infinity of Silence and Voidness. Each object is thus transparent. Everything has its own special inner character, its own karma or 'life in time', but at the same time there is no place where there is emptiness, where one object does not flow into another.*

5 *The least expression of weather variations, a soft rain or a gentle breeze touches me as a – what can I say – miracle*

of unmatched wonder, beauty and goodness. There is nothing to do; just to be is a supremely total act.

6 Looking into faces, I see something of the long chain of their past existence, and sometimes something of the future. The past ones recede behind the outer face like ever-finer tissues, yet are at the same time impregnated in it.

7 When I am in solitude I can hear a 'song' coming forth from everything. Each and every thing has its own song; even moods, thoughts and feelings have their finer songs. Yet beneath this variety they intermingle in one inexpressible vast unity.

8 I feel a love which, without object, is best called lovingness. But my old emotional reactions still coarsely interfere with the expressions of this supremely gentle and effortless lovingness.

9 I feel a consciousness which is neither myself nor not of myself, which is protecting or leading me into directions helpful to my proper growth and maturity, and propelling me away from that which is against growth. It is like a stream into which I have flowed and joyously is carrying me beyond myself.

The Buddha within

When Buddhists meet, greetings are exchanged, the palms are held together like a lotus flower, there is a mindful bow, a moment's inbreath and the silent mutual repetition of the words, 'a lotus for you Buddha to be'. In this beautiful encounter we find a profound acknowledgement; the seeds of awakening are present and Buddha is present in the other. How we see ourselves is crucial. Our self-image is vital to the person we take ourselves to be. Low self-esteem breeds a sense of unworthiness. High self-esteem brings self-worth. What self-estimation can surpass the divine? Identifying ourselves with the highest and the eternal is not presumptuous but a deep spiritual affirmation.

10

bodymind – the new paradigm

Meditation has served monastic generations through the centuries, but it is now serving the wider community. Its long incubation in secluded environments has resulted in a mental discipline with the power to astound modern scientific thinking. In this new fusion, Western empiricism meets Eastern mysticism while technology observes consciousness observing consciousness. This interplay of mind and machine will undoubtedly further our present understanding of the ways in which the brain responds to thought; the nature of consciousness remains an unsolved conundrum. Moreover it is highly likely that such research will produce specific practical applications as brain power is harnessed by technology to meet physical problems. In this collaboration between the monastic and scientific community, the ancient practice of meditation is laid bare by expert minds for expert minds. This scientific validation invites you to take the first step and, with a beginner's mind, embark on the journey of a lifetime.

The physical brain

The fabric of the brain has been discovered within the last 150 years.

The Oxford Companion to the Mind

Exploration and discovery never cease; new frontiers always beckon. Each breakthrough changes the view we hold of ourselves and the world in which we live; prevailing certainties invariably give way to a new paradigm. The Victorians looked at the shape of the head to explain how the mind worked; we are able to watch the brain at work: phrenology has given way to neuroscience. We now stand at the dawning of a new understanding of mind, brain and body: the bodymind is the new frontier.

The brain is a remarkable physical organ, a living computer which directs thoughts, memories, behaviours and moods. It co-ordinates the five senses, constantly reviewing all stimuli from the internal organs and the surface of the body, making minute and precise adjustments continuously.

Everything we associate with human culture – values, beliefs, social organization, artistic creativity and scientific understanding – has its roots in our ability to process and reorder the external world through the mediation of the brain; no computer can match its capabilities. Even though the human brain can be dissected, measured, observed, recorded and analysed, consciousness that arises from the activity of the brain remains invisible and elusive: here is the ultimate conundrum.

Describing the bare physical anatomy of the brain cannot answer the greatest mystery of our human nature – where are we to be found as unique individuals in the neural architecture of electrical pulse and synapse?

The chemical brain

Absolutely anyone – regardless of time, mood or previous experience – can create a sense of well-being and build a lasting

foundation for all other forms of personal development.
Whenever you want – in the midst of family pressure, anxious
colleagues, an urgent crisis or seemingly unbearable stress –
you can trigger the production of your endorphins, feel better
and once again sense the good things of life.

William Bloom, *The Endorphin Effect*

The electrical activity of the brain cannot be separated from
its partnership with the brain's chemical processes. The brain
produces more than 50 identified active drugs, and chemical
reactions take place every second, creating a finely orchestrated
interplay that directly affects mood, behaviour and health. Specific
changes in brain chemistry produce specific changes in behaviour.
Breakthroughs in scientific and medical understanding are both
exciting and important as new possibilities and applications take
shape. The discovery of the endorphin marks another frontier in our
understanding of the bodymind.

As with so many discoveries, endorphins were discovered
almost incidentally by scientists researching drug addiction.
Investigating why the human brain contained receptors for
chemicals produced by a plant, the opiate-producing poppy, it
was discovered that the brain produces its own neurochemicals
that share the same receptors. Termed 'endogenous morphine', a
new term entered chemical vocabulary, the endorphin – morphine
produced within the body itself. Produced by the pituitary gland
and the hypothalamus, the body's own morphine, the endorphin,
can produce analgesia and a sense of well-being. Four distinct
groups of endorphins have been identified so far: alpha, beta,
gamma and sigma. Probably evolved through the millennia of
human evolution, this natural body chemistry is related to the
fight or flight syndrome and our ability to endure pain and
trauma.

It is currently believed that endorphins produce four key
effects on the bodymind: enhancing the immune system, relieving
pain, reducing stress and postponing the ageing process. In other
words, endorphins are good for you. Originally, it was thought

that endorphin production was restricted to the brain, but in the 1980s it was discovered that they were secreted throughout the whole system, once again affirming the unity of mind and body. Endorphins can be produced at any location in the body to flow through the whole system like waves in an ocean; the body's nervous system, immune system and endocrine system are all intimately interlinked.

Here is a revolutionary perspective: 'the mobile brain' – a seed thought worthy of meditation. Pert suggests life enhancing strategies to maximize the endorphin effect: 'becoming conscious, daily relaxation, enjoyable exercise, "pointless" recreational activities, tapping into our dreams, guiltless goofing off, experiencing pleasure in little things, public and private displays of affection, sex without guilt, greater laughter and additional sources of merriment'. Endorphins are naturally produced by a wide range of emotional, mental and physical triggers, including exercise, laughter, deep breathing, meditation, massage, music, and most subtly by our states of mind. Studies have shown that chronic stress, anger and depression cause the body to manufacture chemicals that inhibit the healing process and shorten life expectancy; euphoria protects us from stress, illness and premature death. So chose euphoria, choose endorphin!

The emotional brain

The revolution we call mind-body medicine was based on this simple discovery: wherever a thought goes, a chemical goes with it.

Deepak Chopra, *Holistic Revolution – The Essential New Age Reader*

The physical brain reflects a long evolutionary development. Our rational thought processes belong to the neocortex, the newest area of the brain, but rationality is a relatively young acquisition; reflection before action remains a finely balanced ability that can be swamped by emotional triggers from older instinctual processes within the brain.

Daniel Goleman is one among a new breed of commentators: highly qualified in Western psychology, while simultaneously in dialogue with Eastern Buddhist experience. His several works have introduced a Western audience to a new concept, namely Emotional Intelligence (EQ). Strategies for fostering EQ may appear new to the institutions now implementing such programmes with gusto, but in truth, the nuts and bolts of EQ are familiar to all spiritual practitioners. The age old meditative techniques – self-awareness, mindfulness, detached self-witnessing, conscious breathing, practical ways of approaching the emotions and the mind, the principles of moral responsibility and the development of compassion – have become the building blocks of a Western newly-discovered EQ and its twin Spiritual Intelligence (SQ).

EQ provides the antidote to the impulsive action spurred by the alarm system. A moment of conscious detachment enables us to stop, reflect and reason, thereby putting a brake on the super highway between the amygdala and frontal lobe. Communication between the emotional and the reasoning brain is maintained via the neurotransmitter serotonin. Optimum levels permit healthy, normal communication but anger especially burns up serotonin very quickly. Is it merely coincidental that according to Buddhism anger is among the root delusions? Optimal levels of serotonin also bring increased self-confidence, self-control and calmness of mind. Optimal levels are maintained by holding a positive mental attitude to all life experiences; it is impossible not to be reminded of the Buddhist view: equanimity in all things. Meditative traditions offer a wisdom gained over centuries – who would not wish to listen and benefit?

The electrical brain

How does the brain work – what does it actually do? These questions have fascinated and challenged countless human beings over many centuries. At last, we now have the expertise to tackle what might arguably be regarded as the final frontier in human understanding.

Susan Greenfield, *The Human Brain*

The brain is electrochemical in nature. In this amazing wonderland, the neuron conducts a tiny electrical gradient across individual cell membranes signalling to other neurones or muscle tissue.

Magnified billions of times, this transaction permits every action and thought that we take. The electrical nature of the brain was first realized towards the end of the nineteenth century, but the invention of the EEG (electroencephalogram) recorder in 1929 permitted the invisible electrical landscape of the brain to become visible. Early researchers were limited by the slow visual interpretation of the raw data. It was not until the mid-1960s that computer analysis permitted EEG data to be separated into various frequency bands called Alpha, Beta, Delta and Theta.

Brain wave frequency correlates to mental states or types of activity. The Delta frequency is associated with the very young and is seen in deep sleep. The Theta frequency is associated with drowsiness, childhood and adolescence. Theta waves can be seen during states such as trances, hypnosis, deep daydreams, lucid dreaming, light sleep and the preconscious state just upon waking, and just before falling asleep. The Alpha frequency is characteristic of a relaxed but alert state of consciousness best detected with the eyes closed. Low amplitude Beta with multiple and varying frequencies is often associated with active, busy or anxious thinking and active concentration. High amplitude Beta can be related to anxious alertness.

Meditation and neuroscience

What we found is that the trained mind, or brain, is physically different from the untrained one.

Richard J. Davidson

Meditation is ancient, neuroscience is contemporary. Unexpectedly, the two fields are now to be found in unusual liaison; both share common territory in the abiding quest to understand mind, brain and consciousness. This entirely new and recent possibility renders the invisible visible as meditative practice can be seen impacting into the neural network.

The technical and the spiritual together are now making it possible to observe the meditative mind at work. The correlation between mental activity and brainwave patterns has been known since the 1960s. This key finding did much to fuel a cultural revolution centred on the spiritualization of values along with the introduction of practical meditative principles such as positive affirmation, visualization, relaxation and techniques for mindfulness. Now, further research has refined the original conception and moved the ensuing debate to a new plateau: biofeedback has moved into neurofeedback.

Meditation may appear to be a passive process, but in fact it is uniquely dynamic, creating greater levels of consciousness along with both short- and long-term neural change. Functional MRI has revolutionized brain research, making it possible to map changes in the brain. At the Laboratory for Affective Neuroscience and the W.M. Keck Laboratory for Functional Brain Imaging and Behavior in the United States where Buddhist meditation meets Western technology, the old notion of neuroplasticity has been reinvigorated. The term refers to the brain's ability to change its structure and function. Previously thought to be a characteristic only of the very young, it is now clear that the brain has the capacity to develop new neural connections throughout life. Clearly the neuroplasticity of the brain permits recovery from injury and disease, however, it now seems that this ability also responds to internal mentally-generated signals. Davidson and his team have correlated emotional states and brain activity, finding that states of happiness, enthusiasm and joy show up as increased activity on the left side near the front of the cortex, while states of anxiety and sadness show as increased activity on the right. This pattern appears in infants as young as ten months, in toddlers, teens and adults. Researchers at Wisconsin University have been able to render the mental experiences of meditation into the scientific vocabulary of high-frequency Gamma waves and brain co-ordination but, translated into everyday language, this is the impact of mind upon matter. In Davidson's words:

> *What we found is that the long-time practitioners showed brain activation on a scale we have never seen before. Their mental practice has an effect on the brain in the same way golf or tennis practice enhances performance. It demonstrates that the brain is capable of being trained and physically modified in ways few people can imagine.*

The brain, like the rest of the body, can be altered intentionally.

The whole life – the happy life

> *Relax, rejuvenate, energize. Most of all enjoy being in the beautiful, healthy body that you have helped create for yourself, now and for the rest of your life.*
>
> Susan Levy and Carol Lehr, *Your Body Can Talk*

The holistic life is the whole life, and it can be the happy life. Recognizing the interplay of mind and body, thought and feeling, heart and soul is to acknowledge the essential unity of being.

The Western mind seems to have come to this realization only lately, whereas the older meditative mystical traditions have taken this relationship to be self-evident. The West, almost alone, discarded this sense of wholeness and only now, after centuries of estrangement, does it feel obliged to apply the full panoply of scientific weight so that it might not just believe but also understand. When the West's view of the bodymind undergoes sufficient revision, then it will have crossed the barrier between separation and holism. The West most often adopts practical goals; improved health and stress management means less absence at work, greater productivity and less burden on the health services. Such pragmatic goals serve the individual too. This practical approach has already served to take meditation practice out from the temple or ashram and place it in the workplace, the community centre, even in the school. Such new initiatives continue to spread as a more holistic philosophy enters the worlds of business, health and education, worlds that measure success not by personal subjective experience but by hard and fast criteria of goal-orientated targets. The divide between the spiritual and the secular, once seen as a chasm, is being bridged by individuals, institutions and organizations.

Empirical evidence has discovered what spiritual tradition has always known, namely that a dynamic correlation exists between mind and body. The coming together of science and mysticism creates a fascinating union between the East and West. The holistic health revolution is still unfolding; the bodymind frontier is revealing a new realm of extraordinary interaction and marvellous complexity. Holism, the inner secret of all sacred traditions, is here to stay, dressed in a new form for the twenty-first century – the bodymind.